AF470568

HARRIER
AT WAR

HARRIER
AT WAR

Alfred Price

LONDON
IAN ALLAN LTD

Contents

First published 1984

ISBN 0 7110 1441 8

Published by Ian Allan Ltd,
Shepperton, Surrey; and printed by
Ian Allan Printing Ltd at their
works at Coombelands in
Runnymede, England.

Front cover, top:
**Harrier GR3s of No 1 Squadron
moving away fast and low, after
an attack during the Falklands
Conflict in the spring of 1982.
Painted by Flt Lt Roger Green, the
original hangs in the Officers'
Mess at RAF Wittering.**
**A signed print of the painting,
size 17in×25in, can be purchased
from Flt Lt Roger Green, Officer's
Mess, RAF Wittering,
Peterborough PE8 6HB.**

Front cover, bottom:
**Sea Harrier FRS1 of No 800
Squadron.** *Bob Downey*

The South Atlantic conflict in the spring of
1982 gave the Sea Harrier the opportunity to
prove itself in fighter-versus-fighter combat.
This type of engagement is the most com-
petitive aspect of air operations, and will
mercilessly expose any weakness in the
capabilities of an aircraft type or the pilots
flying it. As it was the only interceptor to
enter service since the late 1950s unable to
exceed the speed of sound in level flight at
any altitude, before the conflict the Sea
Harrier had plenty of detractors — this
author included. Many had dismissed the aircraft as a limited capability fighter — able to
drive away slow and large reconnaissance
aircraft shadowing a Task Force, but quite
unable to survive against reasonably modern
enemy fighters. Certainly the Sea Harrier had
a unique ability to take off from and land
back on relatively small carriers, but what
difference would that ability make when they
had to confront high performance
adversaries in combat?

The fighting around the Falklands proved
a lot of people wrong about the Sea Harrier,
and this author numbers himself amongst
them. From the first day they went into
action, the 20 Sea Harriers initially in the
South Atlantic established air superiority
over the Argentine Air Force and Naval Air
Arm and never lost it — even though their
opponents possessed many more fast jet
aircraft some of which (in the brochures
at least) had greatly superior perfor-
mances.

So, what advantages did the Sea Harrier
force possess? The most important single
factor of all was the sound training given to
the British pilots beforehand: they had been
well schooled not only in how to fly their aircraft, but also in the tactics to enable them to
exploit to the full any given combat situation.
A further major advantage to the Sea Harrier
was that it carried the relatively new AIM-9L
version of the Sidewinder infra-red homing
missile, which proved extremely reliable and
effective throughout the conflict.

Introduction

Those were the external factors, for the rest we must look to the Sea Harrier itself. In fact certain important advantages for air combat do stem from the aircraft's V/STOL (Vertical and Short Take-Off and Landing) ability, and collectively these overcome many of the disadvantages of being unable to fly at supersonic speeds. At full power the thrust from the Sea Harrier's Pegasus engine exceeds the weight of the aircraft, giving it an initial acceleration and climb performance only the very latest fighters can match. The V/STOL capability also brought with it the much-publicised ability to use VIFF (thrust Vectored In Forwards Flight), to prevent an enemy aircraft from getting into or remaining in a firing position. Significantly, VIFF was *never* used in combat over the South Atlantic; but afterwards Argentine pilots stated that because of it they were unwilling to 'mix it' with the British fighters and this restricted their range of options in combat.

Other advantages stem indirectly from the Sea Harrier's V/STOL design. Because it uses engine thrust to provide lift during take off, the aircraft's wing is significantly smaller than that of other fighters. In fighter-versus-fighter combat it is an advantage to be flying the smaller aircraft, because the larger aircraft is the more likely to be seen first — and he who detects his enemy first has the initiative in any combat which follows. The Pegasus turbofan puts out relatively little smoke (another factor in making the aircraft difficult to see) and at full throttle its rate of fuel consumption is considerably less than that of any fighter engine running in afterburner (which means the Sea Harrier can usually continue a fight longer than its opponent). The infra-red signature from the Sea Harrier is much smaller than that from an aircraft using afterburner. Also its unique configuration, of a high wing above the four jet nozzles, means that if the pilot banks his aircraft to turn into the direction of the threat — the usual combat manoeuvre when a fighter comes under attack — his wing will automatically shield the hot nozzles and further reduce the Sea Harrier's infra-red signature in the direction of the enemy. These factors make the Sea Harrier (and also the Harrier) a difficult target for infra-red homing missiles, especially if decoy flares are being fired to seduce the missiles away from their target.

A further advantage stemmed from the essential simplicity and maintainability of the Sea Harrier, factors which Dr John Fozard and his team had designed into the aircraft from the start. This had important results during the South Atlantic conflict. In time of war the combat capability of an air arm is measured by the rate at which it can fly effective sorties against the enemy, rather than the number of aircraft it possesses. Unserviceable aircraft, however brilliant their potential performance, contribute nothing to a combat capability. During the most critical phase of the South Atlantic conflict, from the initial British landings at San Carlos on 21 May 1982 until the time the beachhead was secured on evening of the 25th, the force of Sea Harriers and Harriers available to the Task Force — numbering 31 at the beginning of the period and 29 at the end — flew some 300 sorties. During the same period the Argentine Air Force and Navy attack squadrons, with more than twice as many aircraft, flew only 180 sorties of which 117 reached their designated target areas. The Sea Harriers and Harriers flew an *average* of two sorties per day for *every* aircraft in the theatre, a remarkable feat which speaks volumes for the maintainability of the aircraft and the skill and hard work of those who had to repair any battle damage and keep them flying.

During the South Atlantic conflict Sea Harriers destroyed a total of 27 enemy aircraft in the air and on the ground, and Harrier GR3s destroyed four more on the ground, without loss to themselves in air-to-air combat. In each case these figures are substantiated by information from

Argentina. The jump-jets had shown that not only could they survive in combat, but they could go beyond that to seek battle with enemy fighters and defeat them. In doing so the Sea Harrier caught the imagination of the British public, like the Spitfire some 40 years earlier.

The Royal Air Force Harrier GR3s operated against the enemy only in the ground-attack role, often in the face of heavy anti-aircraft fire. Here, too, the aircraft's small size was an advantage; it helped pilots to maintain surprise as they ran in at low altitude, and when they were fired at with automatic weapons the Harrier presented a difficult and fleeting target. During such operations it was inevitable that aircraft would take hits, but the Harrier GR3 came well out of this baptism of fire. In every instance when Harriers were able to return to their carrier with battle damage, this was repaired using the limited engineering facilities on HMS *Hermes* and the aircraft returned to flying. Usually repairs were made during the turn-round between sorties, but even when there was severe damage the repairs never took more than three days. Three Harrier GR3s were shot down by ground fire, but in no case was one lost where a conventional attack aircraft would have survived similar damage.

This book tells the story of the Harrier and the Sea Harrier, from the beginning to the end of the Falklands conflict. In writing it I enjoyed the generous assistance of several people who, in the course of their careers, had been able to view the evolution or operations of the aircraft from unique vantage points: Dr John Fozard, Mr Bill Bedford, Wg Cdr Fred Towern RAF, AVM Ken Hayr RAF, Col Drax Williams USMC, Cdr Nigel ('Sharkey') Ward RN, Flt Lt Dave Morgan RAF, Lt Steve Thomas RN, Flt Lt Tony Harper RAF, Flt Lt Jeff Glover RAF, Flt Lt Eric Annal RAF and Wg Cdr Peter Squire RAF. I should like to express my gratitude to these gentlemen for making it possible for me to write this book and use photographs from their private collections. Other photographs were kindly made available by Lt-Cdr Rupert Nichol RN, Flt Lt Roger Robertshaw RAF and John Godden and his colleagues at British Aerospace, Kingston Division.

Alfred Price
Uppingham,
Rutland

The First Vertical Take-Off and Landing Jet Fighter

The world's first vertical take-off and landing jet fighter to go into service: the German Bachem 339 Natter. This target-defence interceptor took off from an 80ft high vertical ramp. Powered by a 4,400lb-thrust liquid fuel rocket and four 1,100lb thrust solid fuel boosters, it had an initial rate of climb of over 37,000ft/min. The boosters gave thrust for 10 seconds and were then jettisoned. The fighter was to climb to the altitude of the enemy bombers, usually at 20,000-25,000ft, where it levelled out and carried out a single-pass attack during which the pilot was to fire a battery of 24 unguided rockets with high explosive warheads into the bomber formation. Having completed his attack the pilot was to shut down the rocket motor and, when the Natter had slowed sufficiently, bail out. A parachute attached to the rear fuselage would bring the rocket fighter down slowly, and land it vertically. Shortly before the end of the war 10 Natters were readied for action on launchers at Kirchheim near Stuttgart, but before the weapon could be used Allied ground forces neared the area and the rocket fighters were blown up to prevent their falling into enemy hands. The photographs were taken during test flights.

Dr John Fozard entered the aircraft industry in 1943, when he joined Blackburn Aircraft Ltd as an indentured apprentice. After gaining his external degree in engineering from London University, and a postgraduate diploma from the College of Aeronautics at Cranfield, in 1950 he joined Sir Sydney Camm's design team at Hawker Aircraft Ltd, Kingston. In the years that followed he worked for the company on numerous design projects for advanced military aircraft and in 1965 he became the Chief Designer leading the team responsible for the fighter attack aircraft which, in 1967, received the name Harrier.

Although initially he was not directly involved with the design work on the P1127, John Fozard's desk in the Project Office at Kingston was next to Ralph Hooper's who led the group responsible for the early development of the aircraft. The two men worked side by side, each following the progress of the other's work. The most important point to decide, in designing a jet V/STOL aircraft, is the engine configuration. Relatively quickly, the field of possibilities was reduced to two alternatives: an aircraft with a single large engine with rotating nozzles to vector the thrust to provide lift; or an aircraft with separate engines, one for forward flight and others to provide lift. On this decision, John Fozard recalls:

'I was doing project design studies on other configurations. We were looking at lift-engine solutions and other things as well. We have several "wallpaper books" of what we call "funny configurations", many of which were far more unbelievable than the one which Ralph stumbled across. But you have to explore all the alternatives, to make sure the one you finish up with is right. Even if you have 10 or 15 years' experience in aircraft design, it is no use just having a "feeling in your water" that a layout is the best possible. To convince others who will be party to your decision, you have to show that you have looked at the alternatives and are aware of their penalties and benefits compared with the particular configuration or shape that you are proposing.

'Early on in the P1127 project the refined configuration — a single engine with four nozzles which rotated to point downwards for lift — began to make a lot of sense. For one thing it was dead simple. It had only one engine, and with one engine it is quite clear: either it works or it doesn't work — and if it doesn't work, your trained military pilot makes a quick grab for the black-and-yellow handle and wins himself a Martin-Baker tie.

'The essence of a multiple-engined V/STOL aircraft, whether it is a twin, a four, an eight or whatever, is that you must be able to survive an engine failure — because with multiple engines there is statistically a much greater chance of suffering a power unit loss than with a single engine. In aircraft like the Dassault Mirage IIIV and the Balzac [the French prototypes which at that time were competing for NATO approval for a future V/STOL aircraft], there were eight lift engines and a separate propulsive engine. If there was an engine failure during a vertical take-off or landing, the problem was how to survive the loss of not one eighth of your lift but more probably two-eighths — because if the lift engine in one corner went out, the pilot could probably not hold the aircraft in trim without throttling back the engine in the opposite corner across from the centre of gravity. So an aircraft with eight lifting engines has its power in 25% packages, and certainly during jet-borne take-off, and possibly the landing as well, the aircraft could not survive the loss of 25% of its lifting power.'

The Road to the Harrier

1

He has no doubt that the decision to go for a single large engine for the P1127, rather than several smaller ones, was correct:

'The essential principle is a single motor that provides both propulsion and powered lift via rotating nozzles. It looked right from the engineering point of view. It made sense. It was simple, there was not a lot to go wrong. All our experience then — and since — is that if a thing is complicated it will go wrong and it will cost more money to develop and test. And when it does go wrong you will lose more aeroplanes and kill more pilots. So avoid unnecessary complication — that was part of the training Sydney Camm gave us.'

The straightforward and relatively undramatic flight trials of the P1127 proved that the concept was right; and in 1963 the company received a contract to build a supersonic V/STOL aircraft, the P1154. John Fozard was appointed Chief Designer of the team working on this project, which called for an aircraft more than twice as fast and nearly twice as heavy as the Harrier would eventually be. Initially this programme was intended to provide a single-seat attack aircraft for the Royal Air Force and a two-seat carrier-based interceptor for the Royal Navy. This dual requirement proved difficult to meet, however, and early on the Navy

Below:
The prototype P1127, XP831, pictured in August 1960 during initial engine runs at Dunsfold in a specially constructed pen, with metal shrouds to direct the exhaust gases down to a grid. Chief Test Pilot Bill Bedford is sitting in the cockpit and Frank Cross, the head of the Experimental Design Office, is on the ladder beside him.
British Aerospace (unless otherwise stated, all photographs are from this source).

pulled out of the project in favour of the F-4 Phantom. Work on the attack aircraft for the RAF continued and its Chief Designer has no doubt that the P1154 could have been made to work. But the resultant aircraft would have been considerably more demanding in its operating requirements than the Harrier:

'The RAF really wanted the P1154, but they weren't prepared to give up anything in the wingborne arena to get V/STOL performance and an off-base capability. They wanted an aircraft that could do Mach 2, with a far greater radius of action than the subsonic Harrier could provide. They wanted a real macho aeroplane. All pilots do, don't they? And as long as air forces are run by chiefs most of whom have come up via fighters, they'll want their young pilots to follow that "Red Baron" experience. And who can blame them?

'Of course, we were in business to give the RAF what it wanted; but I couldn't help feeling that the P1154 was a bit too ambitious — a dauntingly large leap for a first generation V/STOL jet. I was told on more than one occasion by a very senior man at Hawker Siddeley "Look, if the RAF wants a supersonic V/STOL aircraft, Foz, its your job to give it to them. And don't bloody argue!"

'What concerned us most was the amount of energy released beneath the aircraft from all those high velocity jets — the Harrier's Pegasus does not give the sort of exhaust heat and velocities you get with PCB [plenum chamber burning — burning additional fuel in the two front nozzles, to have been fitted to the P1154 to increase thrust]. This would have constrained the P1154's ability to use unprepared bases without steel sheets or concrete from which to operate. Today the Harrier — which has a more energetic engine than the Kestrel, which could cheerfully operate vertically from grass — needs an aluminium mat to operate from. But a supersonic aircraft probably could not use an aluminium mat for vertical take off, it would need to be steel because of the much higher engine exhaust temperatures and velocities.

'With hindsight I am sure we would have got the P1154 into service, scheduled for about 1970. But once the aircraft was in squadron service, I think the RAF would have found all sorts of limitations in off-base operations. I reckon we would never have built more than about 50 or 60 supersonic P1154s for the RAF, and that would have been the end of it. And today we would have a totally different — and much more jaundiced — view of operational jet V/STOL.'

In other words, had the P1154 gone into service, the RAF would never have brought itself to order a subsonic V/STOL attack aircraft whatever the apparent advantages. So the very much simpler Harrier, able to operate with great reliability from the simplest of bases, would never have seen the light of day. All of this remains conjecture, however, because early in 1965 the British government conducted a major policy review aimed at slashing defence spending. As a result, one of the projects cancelled was the P1154. At the time the cancellation hit the company hard:

'When it was cancelled, the first P1154 was about one-third built. There were bits existing for the first four or five aeroplanes. Hawker Siddeley Aviation had about 700 or 800 design people — engineers and technicians — working on various stages of the project at Kingston, Brough and Hamble. And there was an equal number in the Kingston and Hamble works, in the production and engineering departments, preparing to start manufacture. We had quite a lot of people committed to it.'

Although a major project in the British jet V/STOL programme had come to an end, other aspects of it were allowed to continue. Even as the P1154 cancellation was going through, the pilots and ground crews for the Kestrel Tripartite Evaluation Squadron were undergoing training at Dunsfold. In the spring of 1965 the unit began forming at the Central Fighter Establishment at West Raynham. Deprived of the supersonic aircraft it has originally wanted, the Royal Air Force were persuaded to accept a far less ambitious subsonic V/STOL attack aircraft based on the Kestrel. John Fozard was appointed Chief Designer of the team working on the new aircraft.

'We were told that the RAF was not having the P1154, but it did need a V/STOL close support attack aircraft. We were to take the Kestrel and redesign it to a new RAF specification. Basically we took the Kestrel airframe and enlarged the wing and the intakes, we installed an engine developing more thrust, and made it operationally more capable and easy to service. All of this made

it markedly different from the Kestrel, which
was essentially a minimum-cost operational
research aircraft to evaluate the practical
merits of V/STOL in the field. The Harrier
was a more than 90% redesign of the Kestrel.
We changed just about every drawing, there
wasn't much left in common between the two
aeroplanes.'

As work progressed on the Harrier, the
design team found they were able to make
use of many of the features which had been
developed for the P1154.
'Looking back on it, the P1154 was not a
blind alley. We learned a lot from it, and
what we discovered in three years of every
intensive study and wind tunnel and
engineering test work, we fed into the
redesign of the Kestrel to turn it into a real
operational aeroplane.

'The development work done on the
P1154 undercarriage, in particular, was
directly useful for the Harrier. For the
vectored thrust jet V/STOL aircraft we used
a bicycle landing gear, with outriggers on the
wing tips. This was new and we found we
had a lot to learn, and we learned it incre-
mentally. On the Kestrel we didn't get it
right. The Kestrel's undercarriage was only
marginally better than that of the P1127. As
a result the Kestrel was a hairy aircraft to
land, and in crosswinds it was a devil. We got
it right in the change from Kestrel to Harrier.
On the Harrier the outriggers are pro-
portionally very much stronger. We changed
the springing characteristics on the main and
nose gear, which altered the "ride" of the aircraft and made its ground handling better
than that of a conventional fighter. A lot of
that came out of the study work for the
P1154.
'The cliché image of an aircraft designer is
like the movie presentation of Reginald
Mitchell in 'The First of the Few', of a man
poring over his drawing board at midnight
and, apparently alone, coming up with the
Spitfire. This really is a long way from the
truth. He was a *chief* designer with a team
and in my case, on the Harrier, I was the
chief among damn-near-equals in a team.

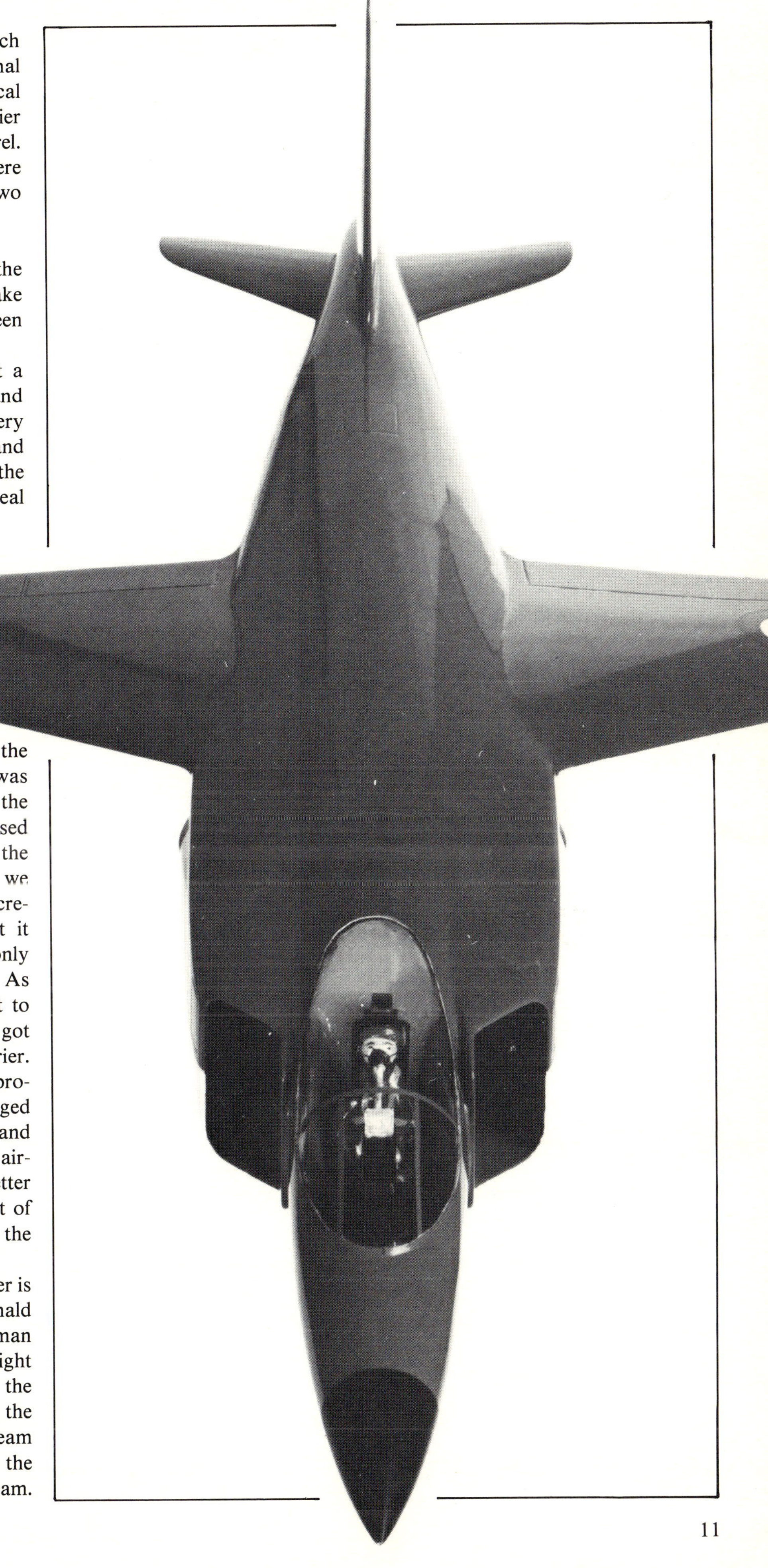

Somebody has to stand in front and tell the team what to do and stop people going off in corners and playing their own tunes. As a Chief Designer I considered my role much more akin to the 18th century Kapelmeister, who sat with the band and led from the middle of it, rather than like that of the modern conductor who stands with his back to the customers in a railed-off enclosure and influences the product chiefly by gestures.

'Very few of the ideas in the Harrier are the Chief Designer's. There are only two or three of the features of the aircraft I can genuinely claim as my own. It was entirely a team effort. Anyone who claims he can design a modern combat aircraft by himself has got to be paranoic. The Chief Designer's job is to orchestrate the whole thing, to oversee the specialist engineers.'

In making the Kestrel into an operational attack aircraft, John Fozard and his team altered almost the entire internal structure. Yet for sound reasons the general external configuration of the aircraft remained largely unchanged. Ralph Hooper and the P1127 and Kestrel design teams had done their work well, and there was little room for fundamental improvement:

'The external shape of an aircraft usually follows the logic of what the aircraft is intended to do. In other words, the form follows the function. Because the Harrier is a V/STOL aircraft the engine — the heaviest single item — has to be on the centre of the airframe so that the centre of thrust coincides with the centre of gravity. The wing centre section has to be in about the same position and, with four nozzles blowing downwards for vertical take-off and landing, it obviously has to be a high winged aeroplane. We could not have a low tailplane, because that would have placed it in the jet exhaust which is not good for tailplanes. So the Harrier had to be a high winged aircraft, with the engine fitted in the centre of the airframe immediately below the wing, and with a high set tailplane.

'The shape of the wing was governed by the speed and turning performance specified, and by the need for it to have sufficient volume to carry part of the fuel. The best wing for turning performance is one with a high aspect ratio, a thin wing with a long span. But this would have been too heavy and it would have given a greater wing area than we needed. So on a fighter or attack aircraft one tends to end up with a short, squat wing. That of the Hunter had an aspect ratio [the ratio of wing span to width] of 3.5, that of the Harrier is about 3. "Form follows function" is a engineering cliché, but it really is true.

'These are the sort of engineering constraints you have as an aircraft designer. You are not free to choose from a mile-wide range of options, you have only little sectors here and there where you are free to alter the shape of your aircraft. And in my case, with the Harrier, this had to be a minimum-risk programme based on the Kestrel. We couldn't mess about with the shape of the aeroplane, even in small ways, because if we introduced aerodynamic changes that had not been tested this would have introduced risks. So, to give an example, we inherited from the Kestrel the original P1127 tailplane with an extension to it. This gave a kink in the leading edge which I did not like, it looks a bit amateurish. We had to strengthen the tailplane but I kept the same aerodynamic shape because that way we knew there was minimum risk of changing the aircraft's flight characteristics for the worse. It was right structurally and aerodynamically, it worked in all senses of the word, so we left it alone. Thus it has remained so until, 15 years later on the AV-8B, it has been redesigned in carbon fibre without the kink.

'In the end there are few things you can do to exercise your personal influence on the *shape* of the aircraft — and I'll give two examples of where I did, one on the Harrier and one on the Sea Harrier. My team had to redesign the outer wing of the Kestrel because we needed to increase the span [of the Harrier wing] by a couple of feet, and I had some influence on the final shape. And the nose shape of the Sea Harrier was entirely done to my "eye requirements": we had to enclose a radar and other equipment in the nose, and we needed to raise the pilot to give a new view line. However, within these constraints the overall shape of the Sea Harrier nose is *exactly* as I wanted it to be. And for me one of the satisfying side-effects is that so many people have said that the Sea Harrier is the first of the breed to look both purposeful *and* elegant!'

Once the layout and external configuration of the Harrier had been finalised, the task of designing the internal structure and systems followed normal practice.

'To work on the internal shape of the aircraft you feed in more and more of the design team, because you have in mind a first-flight date with a drawing-issue programme to meet it. You know what you need to do and work out how you can achieve it within the time-scale. It is all ordered and structured. You have to plan for wind tunnel testing, you have to plan to build test rigs and you have a schedule for the completion and release of production drawings. At this stage of the game the configuration is fixed, you know the engine, what it is going to carry, you know where the fuel is going to go, the basic assembly is all there and defined. Then more design people from outside come in, the works process engineers and the production engineers to build the jigs and tools. Parts are issued to the shops, material is cut and formed, sub-assemblies are made and the whole thing takes on the trappings of a phased process and programme.

'The next big decisions concern the parts that will go together to make up the structure. How is the structure to be built and what materials should we use for the various parts? Should we make them up from plate? Should we machine them from the solid? Or should we use extrusions or forgings? A lot of engineering analysis goes into all of that.

'You have to know what your company is capable of — it is no use asking the production engineers to do something they have never done before, if you want the parts quickly. So you suck your teeth very hard, if you find some piece of the aircraft that demands new manufacturing or production techniques that nobody has ever used before. You would be very unwise to commit your aeroplane to *that*.

'With the Harrier there were virtually no untried manufacturing techiques, because we deliberately avoided them. We had used bonded honeycomb construction before, so we used it in the flaps, aileron and tail unit. We had experience of machining thick plates, so that was the natural choice for the wing skins of the Harrier. The basic skin thickness is about an eighth of an inch, with local areas near the root where the material is much thicker. The main skins of the wing box are machined from slabs of aluminium about $2\frac{1}{2}$in thick. The largest of these plates goes on the cutting machine weighing some 2,500lb and when the computer-controlled operation is complete we take the part we need off the machine weighing about 180lb.

'So the engineering techniques we used in the Harrier were, in the main, those we had used previously though some were used more intensively or with a different scale of

Left:
A full scale mock-up of the P1154, photographed early in 1964 in the Experimental Department at Kingston.

13

Above:
XP976, the fourth P1127, showing permanent buckling of the alloy skinning of the rear fuselage due to the hot exhaust from the Pegasus failing to separate. The problem was not finally solved until, in the design of the Harrier, this part of the fuselage was skinned with titanium.

not come about by accident, they had been designed into the aircraft from the start.

'We planned the aircraft to be easy to service, using all the data we accumulated during 600 to 800 hours of Kestrel flying during 1965. I was determined that we would meet the declared reliability and maintainability objectives on the Harrier. One important thing we did to assist this was to cut a large hole in each side of the rear fuselage, so that the maintainers could get at the equipment positioned there. When the stress people saw what I wanted to do they blew furiously through their beards and said "You can't cut holes *that* big in the rear fuselage!" I said "Why not?" I tried to devise a quick-release shear-carrying fastener, but that would have taken too long to develop. In the end we arrived at a solution where the door itself — made of the chemically etched titanium — is load carrying. It is still a pain in the backside for the RAF and Naval maintainers, because there are 22 screws around the edge of each door — increased to 28 on the Sea Harrier; they would love to have two latches to remove each door quickly. But you cannot have that sort of easy access and still have the door carrying loads.

'We concentrated most of the avionics on two shelves in the rear fuselage. And to get good equipment life we decided to suspend the 450lb of avionic equipment on anti-vibration mountings and feed cooling air to them through the thickness of the shelves, so that it blew stright into the boxes. This helped give the avionics a smooth, quiet and cool ride which greatly assisted reliability.

'We looked at the joints and fasteners around the aircraft, and made as many as possible quick-release. We followed an engineering policy of trying to test, before the aircraft went into service, nearly every removable component, so that we could declare a life that equalled the overhaul period of the aircraft which was then 800 hours. So the minimum requirement for the pieces of equipment, wherever possible, was that unless it went wrong it would not require changing in less than 800 hours.

'Of course, someone has to pay for all of this. The equipment is more costly because you test if more, and you use more units during the tests. But, compared with what the RAF and the Royal Navy would have to spend on extra spares and recycled parts,

application. There was one major exception: we decided we had to replace the aluminium skins on the rear fuselage of the Kestrel because they were taking one hell of a beating from vibration from the engine exhausts, and this was causing acoustic fatigue. We decided these had to be made of titanium of a certain thickness; then we worked out the weight and said "We can't have that!" So we decided we had to use chemically etched titanium (you lay down a pattern corresponding to the frames and stringers to mask off these areas, then you use acid to eat away the metal over the remaining areas, such as panels, which can be much thinner). I think I am right in claiming that the Harrier was the first production aircraft to use chemically eteched titanium sheet. We pioneered the use of titanium bolts instead of steel bolts in the structure. A completed Harrier contains more than 16,000 titanium bolts of various lengths and sizes and this saved over 50lb of weight at a very reasonable cost per pound. These were the only major new engineering techniques we used in manufacturing the airframe of the Harrier.'

One of the things the Harriers and Sea Harriers demonstrated during the Falklands campaign was their excellent serviceability under difficult operating conditions, and their ability to return to base and land even with quite severe battle damage. These abilities did

The Harrier tailplane, showing the 'kink' in the leading edge inherited from the P1127. John Fozard disliked this feature and would have like to have changed the outline, but the Harrier was a 'minimum risk' redesign of the Kestrel and as this might have had an adverse effect on handling characteristics, the tailplane was left as it was.

and in extra maintenance man-hours during the service life of the aircraft, it was a highly effective investment.

'In the vertical take-off mode weight is crucial, so in the Harrier we could afford to pay only a little extra weight in making the aircraft more maintainable; it came to less than 150lb. There were other weight penalties we had also to accept. We added over 100lb to the weight of the airframe to lessen its vulnerability to bird strikes: we thickened the skin on the air intakes and wing leading edge, doubled the thickness of the windscreen, and made the nose stronger.

'We did a lot of studies on the possibility of adding armour to the aircraft to make it less vulnerable to battle damage, but the penalties of adding such weight to a V/STOL aircraft are too great. There are certain fundamental things you can do to reduce vulnerability, however. For example on the Harrier we divided the fuel system into two parts, so that if there is a hole in one part the most you lose is half of the fuel. We also separated the control runs and principal electrical circuits, to minimise the risk of a single hit causing the loss of an aircraft.

'I was not at all surprised that the Harrier came out of its baptism of fire as well as it did. By today's standards it is a simple aeroplane, easy to repair. There are no particularly vulnerable areas, no concentrated load points where if there is a single hit the wing comes off.'

As he looks back on the Harrier, which for all the design constraints is his creation more than anybody else's, what are John Fozard's feelings?

'In some ways I am discontent that I am not allowed to have another go at it, because it is a characteristic of an engineer that he feels he will always be able to do a lot better the second or the third time around. He would like to remould the product, cost and time permitting, always to make it nearer what he knows will do the job better. But, apart from that, I am happy that the Harrier turned out the way it did.

'At the most mundane level, and exciting as aeroplanes are, they are merely pieces of engineering that move. For me the entrancement has always been in dynamic engineering objects such as cars, ships and trains, but most of all aeroplanes. Since I was old enough to remember, I have always wanted to "play" with aeroplanes.

'I believe — though some nuclear engineers might dispute this — that designing an aircraft is probably the most demanding design discipline you can find in today's world. Because of the supreme demands of performance, not only in terms of speed, range and lifting ability but combined with high fatigue life, low weight, safety, low cost and ease of maintenance, all being achieved in a formidably hostile and unforgiving environment, aircraft design has always held for me the ultimate engineering challenge.'

Mr A. W. (Bill) Bedford joined the Royal Air Force in 1940 and flew Hurricane, Thunderbolt and Mustang fighters during the war. After the conflict he became a flying instructor, then a test pilot at the Royal Aircraft Establishment at Farnborough. In 1951 he joined Hawker Aircraft Ltd as a test pilot, and was Chief Test Pilot from 1956 to 1967 during which he conducted the initial flight testing of the P1127, the Kestrel and the Harrier. In this account he gives his impressions of the period leading up to the first flight of the P1127, and the first 18 months of its flying trials.

During his time as Chief Test Pilot Bill Bedford's office was at the firm's test airfield at Dunsfold near Godalming in Surrey. But part of his job was to maintain close contact with the Forward Projects Office at the main works at Kingston where, in 1957, he saw the preliminary sketches of the P1127: a radically new type of aircraft intended to have a vertical take-off and landing capability.

'Sketches started to appear in the drawing office and there was some discreet talk about a new vertical take-off aeroplane. I was brought into the picture at quite an early stage, and asked my views on the concept. Well, I had seen many, many projects over the years that never got anywhere. And I think if ever there was one which I personally thought would not make it, it was this. The Hawker tradition was to go for a concept that has been proved, and to make it very much better. That was Sydney Camm's philosophy. As a company, Hawker was always operationally very realistic. We were not in the business of building research projects.

The line of thought was that in the future airfields were going to be more vulnerable than ever before — and, my goodness, they had been vulnerable enough back in World War 2. So having the ability to operate from bombed airfields, or independent of airfields altogether, would provide an important advantage.

'I am a cautious man by nature, and it took me a bit of time to realise that, slowly but surely, the P1127 project was going to develop into a real aeroplane and I was going to find myself flying it.'

As part of his training to fly the P1127, Bedford underwent a short conversion course on to the Hiller 2E helicopter:

'We thought it would be useful for me to learn the psychology of operating at zero speed, to get used to the idea of manoeuvring in the hover and the visual cues you use for landing on a spot. And one had to get used to rates of ascent and descent, being careful not to generate such a high rate of descent one could not arrest it. It was a very important part of my pre-jet-V/STOL flying training. Also I flew the variable-stability helicopter at NASA in America, and thus got a good idea of the problems we could expect with the P1127.'

On 21 October 1960 the prototype P1127, XP831, was ready to begin tethered hovering trials at Dunsfold:

'We were sufficiently experienced to realise that we had a lot of major problems ahead if we were to get the V/STOL side and the conventional flying side of the aircraft right. It was a new concept, a new engine, a new control system. We knew it was not going to be easy. And we started life with only a very modest amount of thrust — about 10,500lb — which allowed us to carry fuel for only two or three minutes in the hover. Even to achieve this we had to reduce the weight of the aeroplane substantially and we removed the radio set, pitot tube, several fairings and other items.

'We were working on the limits but it was essential to prove the vertical take-off aspect, because that was the major unknown factor of the aircraft. We needed to learn the answers to some fundamental questions. One, would the thrust exceed the weight and enable the aircraft to take off vertically? Two, would the pilot have sufficient control over the aircraft during jet-borne flight? Three, what unforeseen problems would emerge during the early hovers?

'What emerged, very early on, was that the aeroplane was short of control in the rolling and yawing planes — there was not enough "puff" from the wing tips or out of the tail. And in roll the aircraft had too much freedom, so that as I lifted off the ground the main undercarriage oleo extended but the outriggers didn't. The aircraft would lean either to the right or the left, one wing would stay down and then the horizontal component of the engine thrust would drive the aircraft sideways before I could get the wing up; when that happened the aircraft went out of control to the limit of the tethers. I did this for two or three very frustrating days during the early attempts to take off vertically.

'To enable the aircraft to take off with the wings level we added little spring extensions, just a piece of angle iron with bungee rubber attached to it, to each of the outriggers. These were thought up and drawn "on the back of an envelope" one Friday, and put on the aircraft the following Tuesday.

'The extended outriggers overcame the problem, and with them fitted I could lift the aeroplane off the ground and hover it within the confines of the tethering system. At the end of about a month we removed the tethers and I was allowed to hover freely. In fact, I found the aeroplane much easier to hover in free flight with the tethers off than with them on, although during this phase I never went more than four or five feet above the ground.'

The lessons of the initial hovering trials with the P1127 could be summed up as follows: 'We had proved that the thrust exceeded the weight of the aircraft, that there was a measure of control in hovering flight and it could hover without tethers. But we knew we had to improve the hovering qualities of the aircraft before we could proceed much further. Originally the forward pitch puffers moved differentially to provide a degree of yaw control, but that was found to be totally inadequate.'

Before the next series of hovering tests the reaction control system in yaw was altered to one which blew the air sideways, to port or to starboard, from nozzles behind the fin. At the same time roll control was improved by increasing the mass flow of the air out of wing tip nozzles, and fitting a higher gearing between the stick and the roll controls. Together, these changes would make the P1127 much easier to handle in the hover.

Following the initial hovering trials the prototype P1127 was grounded for engineering work, in preparation for the next phase of the test programme: conventional flight with the jet nozzles locked rearwards. In February 1961 the aircraft began taxying trials, which soon revealed that all was not well with the novel type of bicycle undercarriage: 'There was violent outrigger shimmy during our high speed taxying at about 140kts. The

outriggers had been tested to high speed on a drum by the undercarriage manufacturer, and they had not found any shimmy at all. But when the aircraft was moving down the runway at speed, the wheel on each outrigger was sometimes in contact with the ground and sometimes not. And when the outrigger was not in contact with the ground, the damping effect was removed and it was free to shimmy. Then we had an even more serious problem when, as I used the brakes to slow down, the resultant vibration coincided with the resonant frequency of the under-carriage. There was a lot of vibration, and suddenly the main undercarriage leg snapped like a carrot.'

Fortunately the rest of the aircraft was not damaged, but the trial highlighted the difficulties that Hawker and the under-carriage manufacturer, Dowty, would have to overcome. By this time the work on the second prototype P1127 was well advanced and its main undercarriage leg was removed, strengthened and fitted to the first prototype. To overcome the shimmy, the castoring legs carrying the wheels on the outriggers were locked in the fore-and-aft position.

At the beginning of March 1961 the high speed taxying trials were resumed, this time with no major difficulties. On 13 March Bedford took off in XP831 for its first conventional flight:

'During the take-off run my initial impression was of an aircraft with a high thrust-to-weight ratio and good acceleration. But I didn't do anything spectacular. There were several unknown factors which had to be tackled with care, to make sure that we did not endanger the aeroplane unnecessarily. For example, I took off and left the under-carriage down until I reached 500ft, in case there was any big trim change when it was retracted. And as soon as I was airborne I reduced power, to minimise the possibility of engine surge.

'Then I climbed in a gentlemanly way. Initially there were severe limitations with the Pegasus, there was fan blade vibration in certain RPM bands in the early days; for example, I had to avoid having the engine running between 43 to 54% RPM and 66 to 79% RPM any longer than was necessary. Also I had to be careful not to open the throttle too far, because of the risk of giving the engine "indigestion" — getting a "top-end surge". There was a whole list of limiting conditions on the engine, which later would be progressively reduced as it was improved.

'During the climb I did a few exploratory movements of the controls, to see how the aeroplane behaved. I examined each control individually. I applied rudder to see what the control effectiveness was like. Then I rolled the aircraft from side to side up to 45deg, to feel the rate of roll and see what happened

Above and right:
**The prototype carrying Dexion
extensions to the wing
outriggers, which made possible
the first controlled hovers. Still
the restraining cables are fitted.**

Below right:
**One of the early hovering flights,
after the tethers had been
removed. But although the nose
pitot head had been refitted the
aircraft still could no carry a radio
— note the telephone cable just
visible leading up to the port wing
tip. Note also the strakes added
to the underside of the fuselage,
to increase lift in the hover.**

when I centralised the control column. I found that the lateral control was very good. But longitudinally control was not at all good, if I took my hand off the stick the nose would either rise or fall. Also there was a tendency for the aeroplane to tighten up in turns.

'At 25,000ft I levelled out, to test the aircraft's slow-speed flying characteristics. The only real problem of the flight was when I lowered the landing flaps, and found there was a very strong nose-down trim change. I could not trim it out, and had to pull quite strongly on the stick to hold the aeroplane straight. I therefore retracted the flaps and decided to make a flapless landing, rather than attempt to land with the flaps down trying to hold this large out-of-trim force. The flapless landing worked out quite satisfactorily; on touchdown I streamed the parachute and the aeroplane came to a standstill.

'The first conventional flight in the P1127 lasted 43min. Throughout, my aim was to get the aeroplane off the ground, see how the systems worked, find out if there were any major problems, and get it back safely. Considering the P1127 was an aircraft with some unconventional features, it was a fairly uneventful first flight.'

After the flight the flap travel was reduced, and this cured the problem of exercise nose-down trim when the flaps were lowered.

The problem of longitudinal instability would take much longer to solve, and involved several incremental changes in the design of the tail of the P1127, the Kestrel and the Harrier in years to follow. The P1127 would carry this fault to the end of its life.

'The problem of longitudinal stability was one we had to live with on the P1127. You often do in the formulative days of an aeroplane, you live with a lot of characteristics that operationally would be totally unacceptable. But after the initial conventional flying we found nothing that was going to stop us going ahead with the tests to transition from hovering flight to wing-borne flight, and back again.'

In June 1961 the second P1127, XP836, joined the test programme and took over the conventional flying trials. The first prototype was left to concentrate on the hovering and low speed aspects of the test programme. Slowly, carefully, the flight envelopes of the two aircraft were brought closer and closer together. In conventional flight XP836 was taken slower and slower until, using partial vectored thrust, it flew under full control at 95kt, well below its stalling speed in wing-borne flight. Meanwhile the first prototype was making vertical take-offs, and transitioning from jet-borne to partial wing-borne flight at progressively greater speeds. During one of the tests it too reached 95kts, before it slowed back to the hover and made a vertical landing: the gap between the high speed and low speed performance envelopes had been closed.

In the fourth week in September 1961 the time had come to bring together the two halves of the flight profile, and Bill Bedford prepared to take the XP831, the first prototype, through the full transition for the first time: a vertical take off, accelerating to full wing-borne flight. This first transitional flight, a historic milestone in the history of V/STOL, took place on 22 September 1961. The only real surprise about the flight was that it produced no surprises at all.

'I lifted off vertically, and went into an accelerating transition — which proved to be a complete non-event, a smooth change from hovering flight to wing-borne flight without any abrupt discontinuities, followed by a conventional landing. Then my colleague Hugh Merewether went off and repeated what I had done. In later flights we took off conventionally, did a decelerating transition and made a vertical landing. Then we made the full transition both ways, taking off vertically and accelerating to wing borne flight, then decelerating back to the hover and landing.

'I think the thing that impressed us most, even in those early days when we didn't know the aeroplane very well, was how straightforward was the transition from hovering to wing-borne flight, and back again. So many things came together. Before we did it we used to wonder, if we moved the nozzles down while in conventional flight, how long the aeroplane was going to take to slow down. We soon found that when the nozzles were pointing down that destroyed the momentum of a lot of air and produced considerable drag, even without going into reverse thrust. When the nozzles went down in forward flight there was a deceleration of one-third of a g — enough to push me forward into my straps, a much more powerful deceleration than one gets opening a conventional airbrake. And as speed decreased during the decelerating transition it was

perfectly clear when one had to open the throttle to increase jet-borne lift, because the aircraft started to sink. It didn't just fall out of the sky. So one just fed on progressively more throttle to provide more and more jet lift to supplement the declining aerodynamic lift. Beforehand we thought the wing-borne and jet-borne aspects of the flight would have to be fitted together with great precision, but they did not.'

The P1127 had shown that it could indeed take off vertically, make an accelerating transition to wing-borne flight, then decelerate back into the hover to land. Having got that far, one further fundamental aspect of its operating performance remained to be proved: the ability to make a very short take-off. For this the pilot was to begin his take-off run in the conventional way, with the thrust nozzles horizontal and accelerate the aircraft to about 60kt; when he reached this speed, he was to lower the nozzles to 60 degrees from the horizontal and take-off using a combination of thrust from the engine and lift from the wings. As aircraft continued to accelerate the wings would produce progressively more lift and the

engine nozzles could be returned in steps to the horizontal, when the aircraft would be flying conventionally. The importance of this manoeuvre was that if there was a short run of about 300 yards to accelerate the aircraft to just under half the wing-borne flight-speed, this would enable the aircraft to get airborne carrying a much greater load than it could lift in a vertical take-off. The first such take-off took place at Dunsfold on 28 October 1961, just over a year after the first tentative hovering trials of the P1127. Like the accelerating and decelerating transitions which preceded this phase of the test programme, this proved to be another 'non event' and was devoid of surprises.

One fundamental problem which stemmed from the uniquely wide range of operating speeds of the V/STOL aircraft was the near-impossibility of designing an engine air intake that would be efficient at both the high speed and the hovering ends of the performance envelope. Bill Bedford explained the problem, and the unsuccessful attempt to overcome it by the use of a variable geometry intake:

'For best efficiency from the engine in the hover you want a round, rather blunt, type of air intake that will give the air a smooth passage for that regime of flight. For high speed flight you want a sharp intake. So for our initial hovering flights we used a fat bulbous metal intake. Then, for the conventional flying, we fitted the aircraft with sharp intakes.

'When we started doing the early transitions, we left the bulbous intakes on but speed-limited the aircraft to 250kt. This was pending the development of an all-speed intake, which was going to be of inflatable rubber which blew up to give the bulbous shape for V/STOL, and sucked down to give the sharp intake for high speed flight.

'In theory it looked marvellous. But in practice we could not get them to work throughout the speed range of the aeroplane, they were reluctant to suck down properly after take off. Then we had problems with the bags tearing off at high speed, leaving their remains flapping about like a spaniel's ears. We were lucky we never had a bag go down the engine. So we did away with the inflatable intakes and in the end came up with a compromise intake which had some bulbousness with it, but also it was a sharper profile. When we came to look at the differences in performance, it made very little difference to V/STOL performance, and produced just a little more drag on conventional flight.'

Gradually, one by one, the most serious problems of the P1127 were overcome. The test programme continued, to reveal a flying machine that was not only novel in concept but also very simple in both its engineering and its handling.

'As we did more flying in the aeroplane, we realised what great potential it had and how extremely simple was its concept. To have what was almost a conventional jet aeroplane to fly around the sky in, and then with one lever to be able to point the jets vertically downwards to decelerate for the vertical landing, that really was beyond our wildest expectations. And the handling of the aeroplane was so simple, because the puffer system which controls the aeroplane in nonconventional flight was so very simple. You waggled the stick in the cockpit and moved the rudder pedals, and in addition to moving the controls you opened and shut the puffer jets that controlled the attitude of the aircraft when it was hovering or in partial jet-borne flight. So it all came together, and we found ourselves with a machine that was easier and simpler to fly than a helicopter.'

With the successful completion of the hovering, the transitional and the rolling vertical take-off flight trials, the P1127 had carved an important notch for itself in aviation history. Even if the stubby little aircraft achieved nothing else before being consigned to the scrapyard or the museum, it had demonstrated the feasibility of using a single engine with vectored thrust to achieve jet-borne hovering flight, the transition to wing-borne flight, and speeds exceeding Mach 1 in a shallow dive. But as everyone knows, this was only the beginning of a far longer story. Looking back on the all important initial 18 months of the P1127 flight trials, what are the feelings of the pilot most intimately concerned with them?

'I was fortunate to be the man available at the right time for the project to dovetail into my career, so I had my last seven years as a test pilot on this project. It certainly engraved itself on my heart, in terms of the development work that went with it. There was the excitement of seeing the various problems overcome and the aeroplane emerge from a research machine into a full-blooded operational aeroplane in service with the Royal Air Force, the US Marine Corps, and then it eventually went into service with the RN in a role that it is ideally suited to.'

Left:
To provide an optimum shape of air intake for both the high speed and the hovering ends of the performance envelope, P1127s and Kestrels were fitted with black rubber bladders which inflated to provide a bulbous intake shape for use at low speeds. In this photograph the intakes are seen inflated, as Bill Bedford made the first deck landing with the P1127 on HMS *Ark Royal* in February 1963.

Below left:
Although the inflated intakes were satisfactory at low speeds, above 400kt the airflow would stretch the rubber causing ripples, then it would tear away the bladders. Even the application of high suction failed to hold the bags in place, and the idea was dropped.

Below:
Pastoral scene: XP890, the fifth prototype P1127, pictured at Dunsfold on a wet day. Extending above the rear fuselage is the ram air turbine, to provide backup hydraulic power for the flying controls in case of a failure of the main engine driven system. Also visible is a 'pen nib' fairing behind the rear jet nozzle, an early attempt to reduce damage to the rear fuselage panels due to the jet efflux.

Wg Cdr Fred Trowern joined the Royal Air Force in January 1951. His first operational tour was with No 2 Squadron in Germany, flying Meteors on fighter-reconnaissance. This was followed by a couple of years as a flying instructor, then tours with No 8 Squadron in Aden, where he flew Meteors, Venoms and Hunters, and No 234 Squadron in England flying Hunters. At the end of 1964 he was selected for the Tripartite Evaluation Squadron formed to test the Kestrel, a semi-operational version of the P1127, under realistic service conditions. At the end of the trials he received an AFC for his part in them. Afterwards he returned to No 8 Squadron, still flying Hunters in Aden and Bahrain, as commander. He then moved to a couple of staff appointments, before taking command of the Jaguar Operational Conversion Unit in 1978. In 1982 he was Wing Commander Offensive Support on the Joint Warfare Wing at Latimer, and went to the Falklands during the fighting as General Moore's air liaison officer; for this he was awarded the OBE. He left the Service in 1983 to begin a new career in industry.

In October 1964 Fred Trowern held the rank of Squadron Leader and was one of the pilots selected to join the Tripartite Evaluation Squadron forming at RAF West Raynham, for the operational evaluation of the Kestrel. The squadron was commanded by Wg Cdr David Scrimgeour, and other RAF pilots assigned to it were Flt Lt 'Porky' Munro and Flt Lt Dave Edmondston. From Germany came Col Gerhard Barkhorn (the World War 2 ace, credited with 301 victories) and Oberleutnant Volker Suhr. Three US services sent pilots to fly with the unit: from the Air Force Lt-Col J. K. Campbell, from the Navy Lt-Cdr Jim Tyson and from the Army Lt-Col Lou Solt and Maj Al Johnson. It is interesting to note that the only US service which has so far taken a serious interest in jet V/STOL operations, the Marine Corps, was not represented.

'The Kestrel Tripartite Evaluation Squadron started to form at West Raynham in Norfolk in October 1964. Initially we flew Hunters and Meteors, primarily to get the American and German pilots used to the RAF way of doing things. Also we went to Ternhill for four hours' helicopter flying in the Whirlwind. That was very useful, getting us used to going up and down, backwards, forwards and sideways.

'For the training on the Kestrel we moved to Dunsfold, where Bill Bedford and Duncan Simpson taught us to fly the aircraft. There were no two-seat Kestrels, so before our first flights we spent half an hour taxying the aircraft on the ground, moseying round the airfield and getting used to the brakes and nosewheel steering, and moving the nozzles. One problem with the Kestrel's undercarriage was that the aircraft used to lean markedly when it went round a corner, especially if there was a crosswind, as the weight transferred to one of the outriggers. The aircraft had powered nosewheel steering with two authorities, each controlled in a different way. One was a fairly low authority of nosewheel steering for use during the take-off and landing, controlled by a button on the control column; the other was a more powerful steering authority for taxying on grass, controlled by a button on the throttle. Until one got used to it, controlling the aircraft on the ground was a bit like trying to pat one's head and rub one's tummy at the same time!'

Once they were confident they could handle the Kestrel on the ground, the service pilots were allowed to take it into the air.
'My first flight in the Kestrel was on 19 January 1965, with a conventional take-

The Kestrel Experience

3

off and landing. It lasted an hour. My initial impression of the aircraft was that it was very "touchy" compared with the Hunter; it was far less stable, very noisy and it vibrated a lot. It had only about half the wing area of the Hunter, and a quite different system of power controls.

'On my second flight, on 21 January, I did a vertical take off, hovered for a bit and then landed vertically. It lasted only about four minutes but it was very impressive. I remember thinking it was my most thrilling flight since I first went solo in the Harvard. At that time the Kestrel was desperately underpowered for vertical take off — the thrust-to-weight-ratio was about 1.0001:1! You would take off and climb vertically to 100ft at full throttle, and if you used a bit too much rudder [which bled off some of the thrust] or if the wind changed slightly, you would start to descend. However, one week later I found that the short take-off was even more exhilarating and the decelerating transition quite interesting as one passed through all known stalling speeds [for an aircraft in normal wing-borne flight]. We spent January and most of February at Dunsfold, during which time I amassed about 10 hours flying on the Kestrel.'

By the third week of February the initial training phase was over, and the pilots of the Tripartite Evaluation Squadron flew the seven Kestrels then available to West Raynham. There they resumed flying, as each pilot gained further experience in handling the unusual aircraft.

On 1 April, during this early phase of the operations, the unit suffered its first and only aircraft loss. At the time the US Army pilot involved was making a short take-off from the runway at West Raynham:

Right:
XS688, the first Kestrel, photographed at Dunsfold in its original form and wearing RAF markings at about the time of its maiden flight in March 1964. The aircraft has rubber bladder intakes, which would later be removed, and UHF blade aerials above the centre fuselage and below the rear fuselage. The long pointed nose and pitot tube of the P1127 has given way to a blunt nose housing a forward-facing reconnaissance camera.

Below:
XS688 pictured before delivery, with a Hunter chase aircraft. It still has inflatable intakes, but the RAF markings have been replaced by those of the Tripartite Evaluation Squadron.

Below right:
The first seven Kestrels pictured at West Raynham in Norfolk in February 1965, shortly after the formation of the Tripartite Evaluation Squadron. Note that the inflatable rubber intakes have now been removed from the aircraft, including XS688 (No '8') at the end of the line.

'Lou Solt tried to take off in a Kestrel with the parking brake still on, which sounds terribly silly but it could have happened to anybody. He opened the throttle wide to take-off and as the aircraft hurtled down the runway gaining speed, the weight began to transfer from the main wheels to the left outrigger. The aircraft working itself progressively sideways, until the outrigger collapsed. The Kestrel ended up on its side off the left of the runway with its back broken and the engine still running. Dave Scrimgeour, helped by Wg Cdr Harry Bennett and Flt Lt Coulton, rushed over and pulled Lou out of the cockpit — at no small risk to themselves, because the aircraft was lying on its side broken in two, the engine was still running and the ejector seat had been partly moved and looked as if it might go off at any second. It was a very good effort and they received Queen's Commendations for it. Lou was slightly injured and went to hospital, he never flew the Kestrel again after that. The US Army sent Maj Paul Curry to replace him. To prevent that particular error recurring, a piece of metal was welded on the parking brake lever so that when the brake was on you couldn't open the throttle fully.'

Initially the Kestrels flew off the concrete runways at their base airfield, but as the pilots became more confident the training programme became more ambitious.

'We went over to the old wartime grass airfield at Bircham Newton about six miles from West Raynham, and someone cut several mini-runways with a motor mower. We started off with one 300yd long and 50yd wide, and worked up from there. We learnt the meaning of terms like California Bearing Ratio, the standard measurement of the hardness of ground, measured using a device like a pogo-stick called the Cone Penetrometer. We found that we could operate perfectly well off reasonable turf at speeds down to 20kts. Even today they are not operating the Harrier off grass as extensively as we did in the Kestrel, because people have written the rule books since. You know how it goes in the Service . . .

'We also tried operating off aluminium matting, though the ones we used in those days were extraordinarily small by today's standards — our's were 35ft by 35ft (now they are 90ft by 90ft, giving more than six times as much area).

'The Americans came up with an idea for a polyester landing pad for the Kestrel. The

idea was that one had a big bag of this special chemical composition suspended underneath a helicopter, which carried it to the point where the pad was needed. Then the bag was dropped, and as it hit the ground the bag went "splat" and dumped its contents rather like a big cow pat. It would harden up in a few hours, then the chaps could land on it. The chemicals could be mixed in various colours. But these pads were very expensive and in use they didn't last very long, so they were for emergencies only.

'All we were trying to do, at that stage, was see if the concept of operating attack aircraft from grass fields would work. We didn't do anything that was remotely warlike until July 1965, when we started flying simulated bomb, rocket and cannon attacks operating from strips in the Stanford Practical Training Area [near Thetford] in Norfolk. And we conducted reconnaissance missions using the nose-mounted forward facing camera. But we never carried any bombs or bullets.

'We covered every aspect of the aircraft's operations we could think of, including VIFF [thrust Vectored in Forward Flight] to see if we could increase our rate of turn for evasive manoeuvres. As a combat manoeuvre it would swing the aircraft through a large number of degrees very rapidly. But also, because of the peculiarities of that particular aircraft and engine, it destroyed your airspeed — it cost about 100kts per 90deg of turn. And as the Kestrel was rather unstable in pitch you could find yourself going round in a series of jerks — describing a path rather like the outside of an old threepenny piece!'

As well as operating a new aircraft in a virtually untried way, the Tripartite Evaluation Squadron had also to cope with a completely new engine under these conditions. 'Initially we used to change the engines after only 35 hours, and when there were problems this was reduced to 12 hours. Gradually the engine began to get more reliable, though it remained the same old Pegasus Mk 5 and its thrust did not increase by much.

'Operating on the limits as we were, every pound of thrust lost made a tremendous difference to performance, especially when taking off vertically. When the aircraft operated off fields, the engines were forever ingesting bits of grass, etc, and after a while this would cause a loss in engine performance. It the thrust fell too far the aircraft would not get off the ground at all. We found that by running the engine at low revs, and using a stirrup pump to squirt water down the air intake, we could clean the compressor blades and usually restore the original thrust. But the best way to cure the problem of ingestion was to prevent it happening, so we did some trials to find the right speed for landing so that the dust cloud thrown up by the aircraft at touch down remained behind the engine intakes. That speed varied with the hardness of the ground and the texture of the grass. Generally, if we were landing on grass, we had to come with a minimum of 35kts or so.'

In its clean configuration the Kestrel had a radius of action of only about 80 miles, but this was sufficient for these early operations: 'With the aircraft in position at West Raynham, we had all the facilities we needed within easy range. In those days the whole of East Anglia was a low flying area. We had the Stamford Practical Training Area, a large tract of army-owned land we could operate from. There were the airfields at Bircham

29

Newton and North Pickenham where we did our basic grass work, and RAE Bedford and Twinwood Farm beside it where we could do our confined-space operations among the trees.

'With its limited lifting performance, our maximum radius of action in the Kestrel was about 80 miles staying at low altitude. We found we could come back with very little fuel, it was normal to land with 200lb total. (Later, when I commanded the Jaguar Operational Conversion Unit at Lossiemouth, I would have killed any pilot who came back with less than 800lb!)'

In the summer of 1965 the unit began testing the Kestrel's ability to operate from concealed sites in open fields, with the aircraft camouflaged under trees. Pilots learned not to taxi with the nozzles angled down, because this caused scorch marks on the ground which showed up on aerial photographs.

Although engine surges were quite common in the Kestrel full emergencies were rare, and when they did occur the unit's experienced pilots showed they could cope with them. Flt Lt 'Porky' Munro was awarded the Air Force Cross for saving his aircraft in particularly difficult circumstances.

'As he was doing a decelerating transition, coming in for a slow landing, his engine started to break up and the reaction controls became jammed. Now that, for most people, would be fair justification to say "Bye bye" to the aeroplane and pull the ejector seat handle. But "Porky" quietly put the aircraft back into conventional flight and put it down smoothly in a normal landing. It was a superb effort.'

The only other serious incident on the unit resulted from an uncharacteristic instance of pilot error by its most experienced pilot, Col Barkhorn. The resultant crash-landing hurt the feelings of the German fighter ace more than it damaged the Kestrel. The pilot was coming in to land in a small field when the accident occurred.

'He had 301 confirmed victories during World War 2, so he was a somewhat above-average pilot — you could learn from a chap like that. Anyway, Colonel B had had a

Right:
During the late 1960s Harriers frequently demonstrated their ability to operate from ships of various sizes: (Right) coming in to land on the helicopter pad of the cruiser HMS Blake in August 1969; (Far right) a remarkable meeting in the light of later events, a Harrier landing on the Argentine Navy carrier 25 de Mayo in September 1969.

rather frightening take-off in which he just missed some trees, and he was landing 5-10 minutes later in another confined field. In the Kestrel, as you came in to land, you had to put on progressively more power. And the good Colonel, as he got to round-out height, inadvertently closed the throttle. The Kestrel fell like a stone and crashed into the field. I had been waiting to take the aeroplane next, and I rushed over to see what had happened to him. He was standing beside the aeroplane, absolutely livid, and kicking it. I said "Its all right Colonel, its all right, relax . . ." When I got up close to him I saw that he wasn't angry with the aeroplane, he was livid with himself. Then he came out with what has to be one of the world's classic line-shoots: "Fred, do you realise zat eet ees now 302 Allied aircraft I have destroyed . . .!'

'He is one of the finest gentlemen I have ever met. I said to him "I'll have a word with the boss, and see if we can disguise the incident somewhat", but he would have none of it. He said "No, I made zee pigs of it, now I must pay the price." He didn't want the incident to colour the trials report on the aircraft. With that man everything had to be dead accurate. A fine gentleman and a superb pilot!'

During the evaluation the aircraft did not carry external stores until near the end, when drop tanks were fitted to check the aircraft's handling at greater weights. They raised no significant problems.

The Tripartite Evaluation Squadron lasted just over a year, then the unit disbanded. During that period it flew a total of about 960 Kestrel sorties, of which more than 350 were from grass strips.

'We could see that although the Kestrel was underpowered, a follow-on aircraft with more engine power would certainly work. At the end of the Kestrel evaluation we worked up a long presentation on the operational value of the V/STOL aircraft. Our basic conclusion was that the Service couldn't afford *not* to have this type of aeroplane. We had also worked out the concept of a main base and forward operating pads, which later came to be used with the Harrier. Looking back, I am sure that had there been no Kestrel squadron there would have been no Harrier in service — the lessons we learned were that important.'

Now Air Officer Commanding No 11 Group, responsible for the air defence of the United Kingdom, Air Vice Marshal Ken Hayr came from New Zealand to join the Royal Air Force in 1954. He completed the three-year course at the Royal Air Force College at Cranwell and gained his wings, then came two tours on Hunters and one on Lightnings, followed by a tour at the Central Fighter Establishment where he was involved in tactical trials with the Lightning. In 1968 he became an instructor at the Phantom Operational Conversion Unit at Coningsby, and the following year was selected for training at Staff College — a prospect which did not please him at the time because it would mean cutting short what he thought would be one of his last flying tours.

'I explained to the Station Commander at Coningsby that I thought it a bit unfair, cutting short my single flying tour as a squadron leader so that I could get to staff college; but that didn't cut any ice! It was not long afterwards that the Station Commander called in at the Squadron and said "You remember how you were complaining about going to staff college and cutting short your flying tour as a squadron leader? Well, you're not going to staff college. You are going to Wittering to command No 1 Squadron. Be there on Monday, as a Wing Commander"!'

Promotion to acting Wing Commander *and* command of the first Harrier squadron, with the challenge of proving the concept of jet V/STOL operations: that was a much better deal than going to staff college, whatever the potential career benefits from the latter. By this time, October 1969, No 1 Squadron had received its first Harriers and pilots had started to convert from Hunters on to the new aircraft.

Ken Hayr soon learned that he was the third Wing Commander selected for No 1 Squadron within a space of six months. One had been killed in a flying accident, the other had difficulty converting to the Harrier. At that time there were no two-seat Harriers; during vertical take-offs and landings the fledgling pilots received their instructions over the radio, from slightly more experienced pilots watching the proceedings from the ground.

'When I arrived, the pilots on A Flight were already doing their conversion training. Before flying the Harrier all pilots had to do five trips in a helicopter. The object was not to check us out fully on the chopper — we could not start the aircraft, shut it down or deal with emergencies. But we went quickly through hovers, transitions, then we flew into and out of clearings. I did my helicopter flying in a Whirlwind, and for the final sorties the lower part of the canopy and the perspex panels were papered over so that I could not see down any steeper than one could from the cockpit of a Harrier.'

Having learnt the rudiments of vertical take-offs and landings in a helicopter, and hovering flight close to the ground, the prospective Harrier pilots were allowed to fly in their new mounts.

'We started by flying the aircraft conventionally, with a conventional take-off and a conventional landing. The most "sporty" landing in the Harrier is a conventional landing: you come in quite fast, crossing the threshold at 165kt which is the same speed as a Lightning. But then you don't put it down on two main wheels that are spaced widely apart as on the Lightning, you touch down on what amounts to a single main wheel under the fuselage. On touch-down in a conventional landing the Harrier feels unstable, like riding in a wheelbarrow.

Harrier into Service | 4

Left:
XV755 (flown by Air Cdr Williamson) and XV758 (Flt Lt Peter Dodworth) pictured from Ken Hayr's aircraft on their way to Cyprus during the initial proving flight to the island in February 1970. *Hayr*

Below left:
Wg Cdr Ken Hayr leading the Harriers of No 1 Squadron in formation, during the initial squadron detachment to Cyprus in March 1970. As the photograph was being taken the aircraft were jettisoning fuel.

'On the next sortie we made a vertical take-off and landing, which felt very natural. I soon fell in love with the aeroplane and found it exhilarating to fly, particularly in the V/STOL mode.'

As No 1 Squadron converted on to the new aircraft it became clear that there were a few pilots who, while very competent at the controls of a conventional jet aircraft, were unsuited to V/STOL flying:

'There were one or two pilots who experienced a psychological block over stopping in the air. Everybody had to come to terms with decelerating the aeroplane to below stalling speed and sitting on the four plumes of hot air. However, one pilot admitted that every time he put his hand on the nozzle lever he thought "Oh dear, here we go again . . . ' He never got used to hovering the aeroplane, and left the squadron to become a very good Jaguar pilot.'

On New Year's Eve 1969 Ken Hayr received his substantive promotion to Wing Commander, and formally took command of No 1 Squadron.

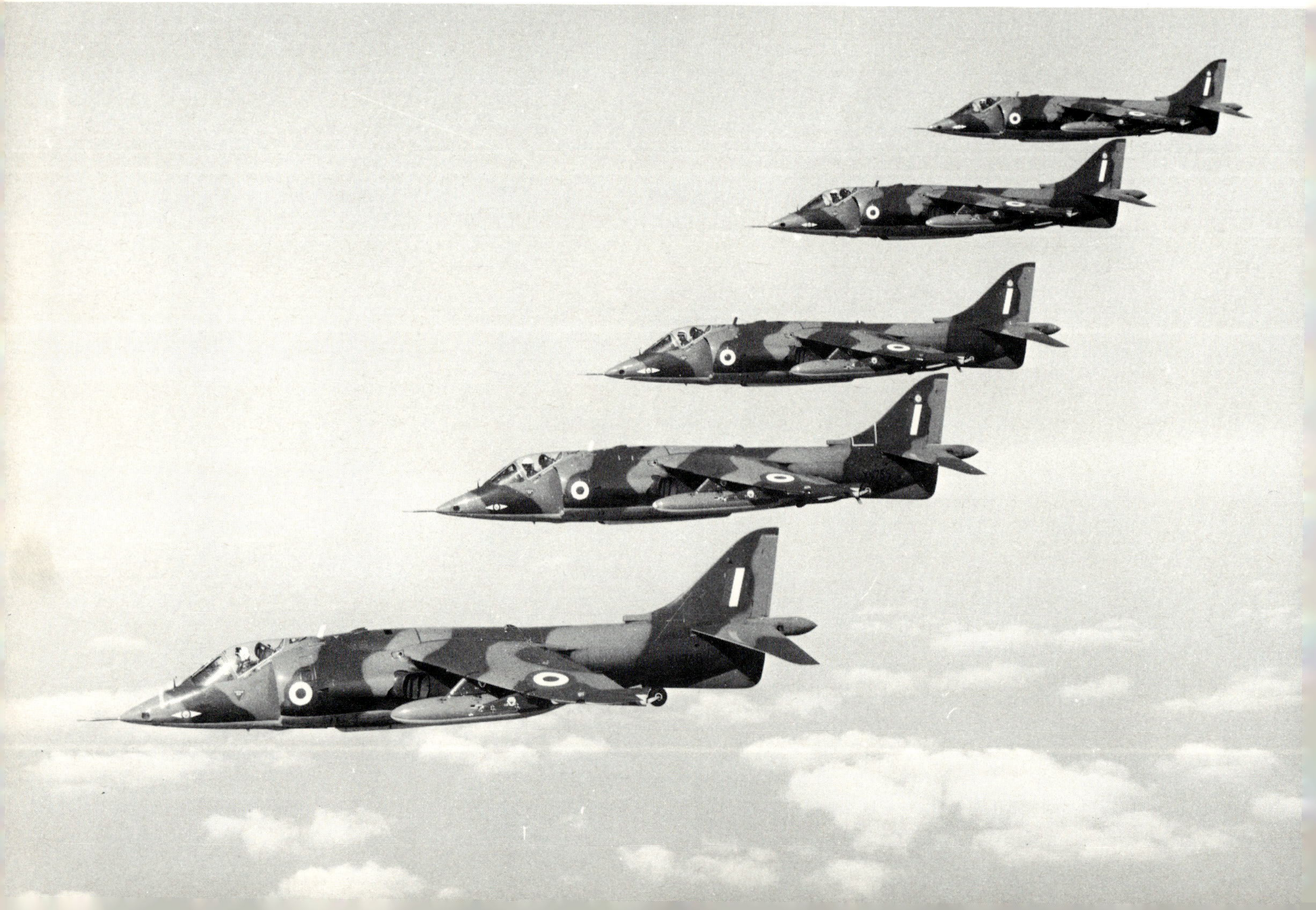

'At that time I was still converting to the Harrier. I had done vertical take-offs and landings, but no slow landings or formation flying. During January 1970 — not a good month for flying — I did V/STOL consolidation, low flying, some instrument flying and then started flying from small pads.'

Also in January No 1 Squadron was reassigned to NATO, as part of the Allied Forces Central Europe (ACE) mobile force. Its designated role was day and night ground attack and daylight reconnaissance.

'Prior to the arrival of the Harrier, some useful trials had been conducted using full-scale Harrier mock-ups sited in what were thought to be typical positions out in the field. Photographic reconnaissance sorties were then flown against these models to see what reduction in vulnerability could be achieved by deploying aircraft away from airfields.

'This experience certainly pointed up the advantages of operating in the field. But nobody had actually done it apart from the original Tripartite Kestrel squadron, and many questions remained to be answered.

Left:
A rare picture of a pair of Harriers landing vertically in formation at Bruntingthorpe near Market Harborough, during the No 1 Squadron detachment in May 1970. The exercise brought to light the danger that if the No 2 aircraft injested hot air from the jet efflux of the leader, it could suffer a sudden and dangerous loss of power close to the ground; soon afterwards close formation vertical landings were banned. *Hayr*

Below:
A No 1 Squadron Harrier taking off from mown grass, demonstrating the value of forward speed to keep the air intakes outside the cloud of debris thrown up by the engine efflux. *Hayr*

The interesting challenge from my point of view was that the squadron was going to be breaking totally new ground; nobody could say to us "That is not the way to operate the Harrier", because nobody else knew.'

During February No 1 Squadron completed its conversion on to the Harrier. The next step was to begin weapons training with the new aircraft, during a detachment to Akrotiri in Cyprus planned to take place in March. But before this move by the full squadron, on 16 February three Harriers took off from Wittering on a route proving flight to the island. At their controls were Ken Hayr and two of the most experienced Harrier pilots in the Service: Air Cdre Peter Williamson, the station commander at Wittering, and Flt Lt Peter Dodworth who instructed at the Harrier conversion unit (and who, at the time of writing, is the Group Captain station commander at Wittering). This was the first service-flown Harrier formation to leave Britain, and when the aircraft landed to refuel at Istres in southern France and Brindisi in southern Italy they aroused considerable interest.

'At each airfield we gave a little demonstration of the Harrier as we arrived: a close formation run-in in Vic, a wing-over, then a stream to long line astern, a high-speed run down the runway, then a turn back, break to down-wind, put down the undercarriage, stream into the hover over the runway, turn towards the crowd, turn away from the crowd, go backwards, go forwards, back into the hover, then land. That was the only way we knew how to land with a formation of three aircraft!'

The three Harriers arrived in Cyprus without undue incident — except that the arrival routine at Akrotiri was flown in the dark! But on the following day, 17 February, Ken Hayr came close to disaster:
'I was flying over the island in a pair with Peter Dodworth when without warning and without my doing anything my aircraft suddenly pitched violently down and up, then resumed flying straight and level. Fortunately we had not been flying very close to the ground at the time. I called Peter and said "Did you see that?" He said "Yes." I said "It wasn't me . . ." So we returned to Akrotiri and landed, very carefully. Clearly there was something drastically wrong with that aeroplane.'

A flurry of signals and telephone calls passed between Akrotiri, Wittering, No 38 Group headquarters at Upavon and the works at Kingston.
'We got in touch with the Company and told them what had happened. After a day or two they discovered a problem with the control system which they thought could have pro-

duced that fault. Control systems are designed so that no single failure of any part of the system should give such a deflection, but much to their chagrin they discovered that there was a critical part in the control system that could put the tailplane hydraulic booster hard over. We left that aircraft at Akrotiri, and on the flight back to Wittering Air Cdre Williamson experienced the same problem in one of the other Harriers.'

The two aircraft returned to Wittering without further incident, but clearly there was something dangerously wrong with the aircraft's control system.
'The aircraft were not formally grounded, but we had to stop flying for about 10 days. Eventually the experts were able to put a finger on the problem. We were told we could resume flying the Harrier, but until the company could design and incorporate the necessary modifications we were not to fly any manoeuvres which involved pointing the aircraft towards the ground (which ruled out almost all of our ground attack manoeuvres), or fly in formation closer than one wingspan.'

The limitations were still in force early in March, and precluded weapons training. In spite of this it was decided to take the full squadron of 10 Harriers and a Hunter T7 on the planned detachment to Cyprus.
'We set off on the 3rd March and flew out via Istres to Malta, where we stopped the night. The next day we went on to Suda Bay, Crete. I wanted to arrive over Cyprus with the whole squadron together, including the Hunter T7. So the Hunter took off first because it was slower in climbing to height. Then I called the tower for taxi instructions for 10 aircraft. The Greek air traffic controllers did not speak good English, and had great difficulty understanding when I asked permission to line up 10 aircraft *on* the runway. We needed only a couple of hundred yards to get airborne, and Suda Bay has a very long runway. So with the first three aircraft I taxied 1,000yd down the runway and the rest of the squadron followed. The controllers were perplexed — they had never seen aircraft line up like this before. I asked for clearance to take off and they said the first three were clear. I said "No, all together." They gave a hesitant "Roger" so I said "Jump formation, rolling rolling, GO!" And we all rolled together and leapt into the air, transitioned into wing-borne flight together and headed off towards Cyprus. That must have given the controllers something to talk about!'

In the clear skies over Cyprus the squadron's pilots were able to fly their aircraft hard, and their experience level on the Harrier increased markedly. Even if weapons training was not possible for the time being there were other aspects that could be practised, including battle formation, air-to-air combat and formation flying (with separations not less than one wingspan). During the detachment the Harrier demonstrated for the first time just how easy it was to keep serviceable:

'In that month the Squadron logged over 300 flying hours, and people thought we had put an extra nought on the end of our flying total. That intensity of flying was completely new with the Harrier.'

In April the squadron's aircraft were modified to overcome the problem with the tailplane control system. At the same time the Harriers were fitted with their inertial navigation equipment and head-up displays units; these had been late in coming from the manufacturers and the aircraft had been delivered without them. Now the unit could resume training for its full role, including dispersed site operations:

'We learned very fast about engine ingestion and foreign object damage — big worries to start with. We learned which surfaces we

could work from, and which ones we couldn't. We went to Spitlegate [near Grantham], a good airfield for grass work, where individual aircraft practised landings and take-offs. The original concept was that we should be based on green fields in amongst trees, rather than on small airfields. However some stretches of grass that we tried were too soft, and we occasionally had to de-bog the aircraft. I therefore argued that we shouldn't try to fly exclusively from green fields and hide under trees: better to go for a harder surface and extend our options by camouflaging the aircraft in amongst buildings. There were those who still thought of the Harrier concept as a green field operation, but no one wants to be up to his elbows in mud if he can avoid it! Although we had a special device for assessing the bearing capacity of natural surfaces, we soon learned to tell whether we could work off grass, simply by digging a heel in.'

During this initial phase of operations the squadron lost its first Harrier, after a bird went down the engine immediately after take off from Wittering. The engine stopped as the aircraft was about 20ft off the ground; the pilot, Flt Lt John Feesey, crash-landed and escaped with minor injuries.

The loss of the aircraft had nothing to do with Harrier field operations, and the training programme continued:

'In May 1970 we made our first attempt at off-base operations as a squadron. First we did a dummy run on the far side of Wittering airfield, camping out overnight with our aircraft to prove that we had the right list of equipment. The next day we got up early, judged the weather suitable and flew a sortie or two. Afterwards, when we knew how many people and how much kit would be needed, we said "OK, how many trucks is it going to take to move that lot?"

'Later in the month we went off base for our first detachment, at Wymeswold [near Loughborough, about 30 miles by road from Wittering]. After two days and nights there we broke camp, put everything in the trucks and went to Bruntingthorpe [near Market Harborough, about 20 miles from Wymeswold]. The Wymeswold site was absolutely bare. That at Bruntingthorpe had been a wartime airfield and there were some old runways; we operated from one corner, using both the runways and the grass.

'During these early detachments we had no proper communications with Wittering.

Far left:
XV753, one of the aircraft delivered to No 1 Squadron when it re-formed with Harriers, ripple firing a pod of 68mm SNEB rockets. *MoD*

This page:
Harriers made for two. (*Above***) XW175, the second prototype two-seat Harrier T2, which made its maiden flight in July 1969. (***Left***) WX270, the sixth production T2 first flew in March 1971; it later served with No 1 Squadron and then with No 233 Operational Conversion unit at Wittering.**

XV278, the third of the initial
Harrier development batch, was
retained by the manufacturers for
trials with various modifications.
(*Above*) With the reshaped nose
which would be a feature of the
GR3. (*Below*) With the Paveway
laser-guided bomb.

Above:
A Harrier GR3 showing the extended nose for the laser ranging and marked target seeker, and aerials for the radar warning receiver fitted to the leading edge of the fin and on the rear of the 'spike' at the extreme end of the fuselage, flying in formation with a GR1A for comparison. Both aircraft belonged to No 3 Squadron based at Gutersloh, Germany. *MoD*

Squadron Leader Bryan Baker, my senior flight commander, would go to the nearest telephone box and ring Air Traffic at Wittering to ask what the weather was going to be like and what diversions they were using. We then flew without talking to anybody else, which is a bit unusual for jet aeroplanes.'

Also in May the squadron moved out for a short detachment to a grass field site at Wakerley Oaks, near Uppingham. While there the detachment hosted several high powered visitors, including the Duke of Edinburgh.

The role foreseen for the Harrier in time of war (and it remains unchanged up to the time of writing) was that the aircraft would fly from a forward operating base (an airfield or a concealed site) some 50 to 70 miles behind the forward edge of the battle area, sufficiently far back not to be overrun if the enemy advanced rapidly. Aircraft would normally operate against targets in pairs, flying Close Air Support missions against targets in the battle area directed by Forward Air Controllers, or Interdiction missions against targets behind the battle area. Typically a pair of aircraft would take off, fly 7-10min to the target, spend a couple of minutes in the target area, then 7-10min flying back to the forward operating base; a total sortie time of 16-22min. Immediately after landing the aircraft would taxi to their camouflaged hides, where they were refuelled and rearmed in readiness for the next mission. In this way aircraft could fly up to six sorties against the enemy per aircraft per day, considerably more than could a conventional attack aircraft based much further from the front line. And the Harrier soon showed that it could operate in weather conditions which would keep comparable conventional attack aircraft on the ground. The number of sorties an air force is able to fly against the enemy, in a given time, is one of the most important yardsticks in gauging its effectiveness in time of war; and in this the Harrier excelled.

At the end of June 1970 No 1 Squadron returned to Cyprus again, to carry out the weapons training originally planned for three months earlier. On the way out the Harriers refuelled at Ciampino airfield on the outskirts of Rome, to give a display before an invited audience. In Cyprus the detachment went off as planned, and included a supported site exercise from the Army Air Corps strip at Dhekalia.

'It was ideal, a 400m tarmac strip used by army light aircraft and helicopters. We found we could just about get a four-aircraft detachment in there. This allowed us to work well forward in the way we had planned, close to the area of operations, so that we could achieve a high sortie rate. We were allocated our own Squadron mess near the beach at Dhekalia, and the whole arrangement could not have been better. Each evening the army forward air controllers would come in, dusty and hot and ready for a drink, and we would debrief the day's sorties. We operated from the Dhekalia strip for a week and found it a very useful exercise.'

At the beginning of August the Harriers returned from Cyprus, and began preparing a routine for the Society of British Aircraft Constructors' display at Farnborough the following month. This was a busy time for the squadron, as it undertook a widely differing range of tasks.

'We seemed always to be on the move. The SBAC display ended on 13 September, and on the 17th we left Wittering for a squadron detachment to Bardufoss in the north of Norway. Up there we did tactical reconnaissance and low flying — it is a fascinating part of the world to fly over. There were one or two problems with the cold, but nothing major. We returned to England on the 27th.'

In the following month the squadron detached to the small airfield at Ouston near Newcastle for live bombing training on the nearby Otterburn range. In the course of this another Harrier was lost when Flt Lt Neal Warton suffered an engine flame-out, following a fuel pump failure as he was on the final approach for landing. He ejected safely.

Now No 1 Squadron's operations settled down to the normal routine for a Royal Air Force ground attack unit in peacetime, and early in 1971 a detachment went to Decimomannu in Sardinia for weapons training.

In May 1971 there was an interesting diversion, when Ken Hayr led a detachment of two Harriers and four pilots to determine the feasibility of operating off the deck of the aircraft carrier *Ark Royal*. Capt Roberts, commanding the ship, took considerable interest in the new aircraft. The Harrier soon demonstrated its unique ability to operate off a deck with minimum fuss:

'During the detachment *Ark Royal's* catapult needed servicing, so the Commander Air stopped fixed-winged flying: "Tomorrow is going to be a servicing day". I asked whether No 1 Squadron could fly nevertheless — we didn't need a catapult. "No, there will be no room on deck." "Well, the lift will will do." The captain relented "Oh go on, let them fly — and give them a splash target!" So we took off vertically, turned downwind, and spent the sortie attacking the target towed behind the ship.

'We also proved we could operate from the deck in worse weather than conventional jet aircraft. There was a day when the weather was absolutely grotty. I was in flying control, Buccaneers and Phantoms were overshooting and the visibility was so poor that you could not see the aircraft as they flew past the island. In the end Flyco said "All

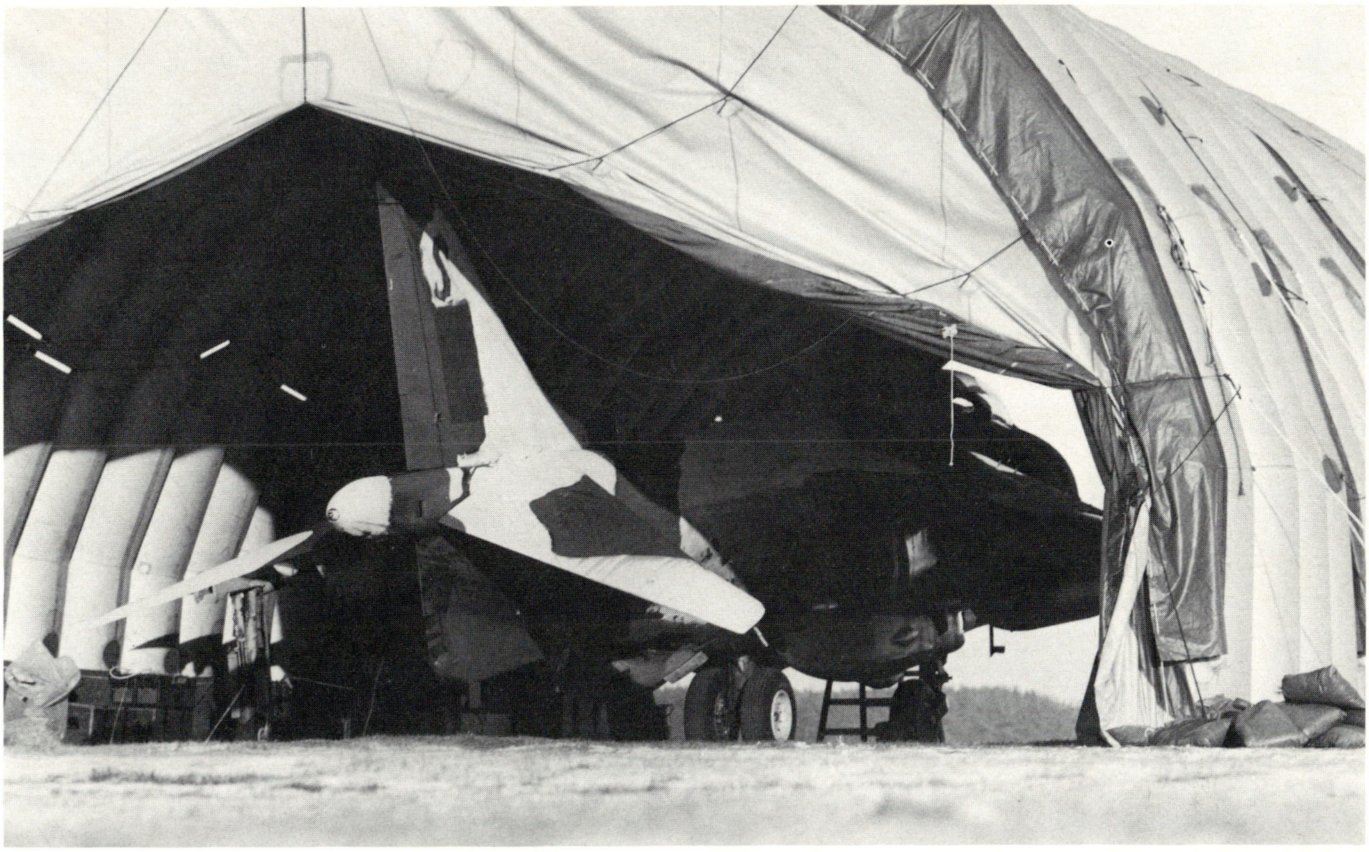

Above:
GR3 of No 1 Squadron at a dispersal site at Virgo Wood on the western side of Wittering airfield. The aircraft is being pushed into its hide by a Mercedes Benz Unimog, the standard vehicle used for field operations with the Harrier; the tanks on the rear of the vehicle contain demineralised water for the water injection system of the Harrier and also provide ballast to give greater traction. *MoD*

aircraft to divert to the mainland". Both of my aircraft were airborne so I said "Couldn't the Harriers just have a go at landing? They have stacks of fuel." And at that moment, out of the mist came a Harrier with the nozzles in the braking stop. Directed by the ship's radar the pilot, Flt Lt Joe Sim, had been coming down the glide slope. He had seen the wake of the ship, gone straight into braking nozzle, and decelerated in time to make a vertical landing. That was another proud moment.'

There followed another detachment, to Oerland in Norway. Then the squadron sent five aircraft and six pilots to demonstrate the Harrier at the Paris Air Show.

On 3 August 1971, after more than $1\frac{1}{2}$ years' operations with the Harrier, No 1 Squadron suffered its first fatal accident on the type. Capt Louis Distelzweig, a US Air Force exchange officer flying with the squadron, suffered a failure of the nozzle control system shortly after take-off. The pilot ejected, but did so too late and was killed. The Harrier force stopped flying for

about a week while the aircraft were inspected and modified to prevent a recurrence.

The squadron resumed its normal flying, developing an air-to-air refuelling capability and bombing techniques with 1,000 pounders. September was spent on detachment at Decimomannu in Sardinia for weapons training, which this time included night ground attack. Then, in distinct contrast, the Harriers went to Gardermoen in Norway during December for an excercise in snow conditions.

On arrival at Gardermoen one of the Harriers was seriously damaged. As Flt Lt Steve Jennings touched down on the ice-covered runway, his aircraft went out of control. Doing about 50kt the Harrier hit a mound of snow and rolled over on to its back. Fortunately the pilot escaped with nothing worse than a severe shaking. The cause of the accident was traced to a failure of the nosewheel steering mechanism, which had frozen up during the high altitude transit flight to Norway. This problem had not previously been apparent, because as the aircraft descended into warmer air the system had

46

time to thaw out. But at Gardermoen the surface temperature was below freezing and when the aircraft touched down and the pilot tried to steer the aircraft, there was no response.

Undismayed by the accident, No 1 Squadron ran a detached site operation with its remaining nine aircraft on the uninhabited side of the airfield.

'The snow was four feet deep but we dug our way in, set out the pillow tanks for the fuel in amongst the trees, and put up our tents. The Norwegians thought we were mad! They came to visit us the next morning expecting to find all of the bodies frozen stiff. But we weren't, and we went on to operate our aircraft successfully for a couple of weeks. We wanted to prove that we could be self-sufficient even in really cold conditions.'

By the end of 1971 the Harrier was fully established in service as a ground attack and reconnaissance aircraft with a V/STOL capability, able to operate with minimal facilities at airfields or field sites between the Mediterranean and the Arctic. Although the aircraft had faced some technical problems, these were no greater nor more difficult to overcome than those experienced with any other advanced military aircraft on its entry into service. And, as is so often the case with aircraft with novel design features, the majority of the problems were not with the Harrier's unique system of swivelling nozzles for V/STOL operations, but rather with systems which the aircraft had in common with conventional jet aircraft.

Ken Hayr's tour as commander of No 1 Squadron ended in December 1971, when he left for his postponed course at the Royal Air Force Staff College.

'I had excellent people on the squadron, a happy bunch of aircrew and groundcrew who got on well. Everyone was proud to be taking the lead in a completely new type of aircraft operation. Nearly every month we were away somewhere, often living in pretty harsh conditions. Looking back at my time with No 1 Squadron and introducing the Harrier into service, it was undoubtedly the most enjoyable part of my career in the RAF.'

Lt Col P. Drax Williams joined the US Marine Corps as a Second Lieutenant in 1963, after graduating from university. As with all members of this service he began his career with six months at the basic school at Quantico, Virginia, learning to be an infantryman. He was then selected for pilot training and learned to fly with the US Navy, where the training included jet operations from the deck of an aircraft carrier. In October 1965 he joined his first operational unit: VMF(AW)-212 (Marine Fighter Squadron [All Weather] 212), flying F-8 Crusaders at Kaneohe Bay, Hawaii. In 1967-8 he flew Crusaders in Vietnam in the fighter and the ground-attack roles, then served there as a forward air controller with an A-4 Marine infantry battalion. On his return from Vietnam he served as a flying instructor, went to staff college, then flew with a Skyhawk squadron. In 1972-3 he returned to Vietnam and flew with a Skyhawk unit based at Bin Hoa near Saigon. Later in 1973 he returned to the USA and joined VMA-231, the third Marine Harrier attack squadron to form, and thus began his long association with the aircraft. Later he commanded the special Harrier demonstration unit from VMA-513, then VMA-542. In this account he draws on his extensive first-hand combat experience of close air support operations, and explains why he believes the V/STOL jet attack aircraft — specifically the Harrier — is the ideal vehicle for this role for the US Marines. He begins with a description of close air support as it was provided for the US ground forces in Vietnam by conventional aircraft, and the resultant shortcomings.

'The Marine Corps had discovered, from its experience in World War 2 and Korea, that most small unplanned battles are decided — one way or the other — within about 30min of their start. And Vietnam was no different. So if the close air support aircraft can't get to the scene within 30min of the start of the action, many times they will be able to do very little to influence the outcome.

'The US Marine Corps is a relatively lightly armed and mobile assault force, it does not have as much heavy equipment as the Army. Our men on the ground rely on air support to give them the extra fire-power they need. So the aim of the Marine air attack units is to provide close air support as soon as possible after the troops request it.

'In Vietnam our bases at Da Nang and Chu Lai were, respectively, about 100 and 150 miles southeast of the DMZ [De-Militarised Zone, the border between North and South Vietnam]; but the 'front line' in Vietnam was wherever the fighting happened to be. Most of our engagements against the North Vietnamese regular army were right up on the DMZ, but there were small guerilla battles in the south all the time. The problem was that, from the time the request for air support originated, it could take up to 40min to an hour before the aircraft arrived at the scene of the fighting.'

There were several reasons for this delay, some due to the over-rigid US Air Force command and control structure used for the control of Air Force and Marine air operations at the time. Often targets were up to 140 miles from the base airfield, necessitating 20min transit flights to reach them. Then there was the problem of having to use aircraft which in some cases were over-complex for the task, and which in every case were tied to the major airfields at Da Nang and Chu Lai, the only two in the area suitable for fast jet aircraft.

'The problem was that if you have complicated jet airplanes with relatively sophisticated avionics like the F-4 Phantom, F-8 Crusader, A-6 Intruder and even the A-4 Skyhawk, you are pretty much tied to a large airfield with an 8,000ft runway. Complicated jets need more maintenance and elaborate avionics workshops, and this means you have a relatively sophisticated base.'

During the most severe fighting, the two major bases in the northern part of South Vietnam could not cope effectively with the vast numbers of take-off and landings required.

'There were too many airplanes going in and out of Da Nang and Chu Lai. At Da Nang we had a big air base, but it was absolutely packed with aircraft. Normally we had four squadrons with about 20 aircraft each on the Marine side, the Air Force had another four with 24 each. And the Vietnamese had a couple of squadrons of Skyraiders. That gave a total of about 200 combat aircraft. Then there were all the Air Force transports, the Army's Caribous and Buffalos, and civilian air liners coming in. On top of that we would get the occasional Navy aircraft from one of the carriers in the Tonkin Gulf, diverting in with battle damage.

'If you came back with an emergency, you could literally be No 4 in the emergency pattern! That was no joke. There could be two or three airplanes ahead of you with battle damage or running short of fuel. If you were scrambled, you could be No 6 in the scramble pattern. There were two runways, one for the Air Force on the east side, one for the Marines on the west side. When there was heavy fighting aircraft coming back with battle damage would often block one of the runways. And the field was constantly being closed by enemy rocket attacks. For two years, Da Nang was the busiest airport in the world.

'The delays in providing close air support were due to the combination of getting air-borne out of the busiest airfield in the world, a cumbersome system of air control, and a 50 to 150-mile flight to the targets depending on where they were. It was just one hell of a long time getting off the ground and up to the targets. And because of this we found our responsiveness to provide air support to the men on the ground, which is the whole purpose of Marine air, was not as good as we wanted it to be.'

The effect of these shortcomings, and the vital importance of prompt air support for troops under attack, was brought home sharply to Drax Williams when in April 1968 he served as a forward air controller with the 1st Battalion, 3rd Marine Regiment during the fighting near Gio Liem close to the Demilitarised Zone.

'On one occasion we received a call at the HQ that one of our infantry companies had run into a severe fire fight and it needed air support. So we went out on an Amtrac [amphibious tracked armoured personnel carrier] through the rice paddies and got as close as we could. Then the fire was getting fairly intense so we went up on foot. I got on the radio and requested close air support, and on that occasion we were lucky. The first two aircraft, Marine A-4s which happened to be in the area, arrived about 8min after the call. But they had already dropped their bombs on another target and could attack only with rockets and guns. Next to arrive were some A-6s diverted from another mission. They each had 22 500lb bombs, and they did the job. They put them down across a tree line 150yd from our forward positions, and after that we had no further problems.

'About a week later, in the same area, we were not so fortunate. We came under attack at about 3pm in the afternoon, and they were able to knock out several of our Amtracs with RPGs [anti-tank rockets]. I put in an emergency call for air support, which I repeated several times. Meanwhile the action became stalemated, we were pinned down behind some dikes on one side of a rice paddy, and the North Vietnamese troops

Above:
AV–8A Harriers of Marine Attack Squadron VMA-542 with in-flight refuelling probes fitted, pictured in camouflaged hides at landing zone 'Bluebird' near the Camp Lejeune training area in North Carolina.

Above right:
Harriers of VMA-231 photographed over Pamlico Sound, North Carolina, soon after the formation of the unit in 1974. Each of the underwing pods contains seven 2.75in rockets.

Right:
Capt John Capito of VMA-542 ripple firing 5in ZUNI rockets over the firing range at Yuma, Arizona, in 1974.

were pinned down on the other side. Nobody could go anywhere and both sides took casualties.

'The first supporting aircraft, a pair of Air Force F-100s, did not arrive until about 5.30pm — *two and a half hours* after my initial request. After that supporting aircraft kept coming and they changed the tide of the battle. The North Vietnamese withdrew and we were able to press on ahead. But in the meantime we had lost 66 dead. We were hopping mad about the delay in giving us air support.

'The point is, response time is critical. If you're tied to large air bases in the rear, you can't provide timely Close Air Support unless you're willing to airborne loiter near the FEBA [forward edge of the battle area]. But that would be prohibitive in the amount of gas burned and, since very gallon of gas has to be carried to the area, you then start adding to the sealift required to support the operation. The obvious answer is to have an attack aircraft able to *ground loiter* near the FEBA.'

Following his return to the USA in August 1973 with the rank of Captain, Drax Williams arrived at the Marine base at Cherry Point, North Carolina, to join

VMA-231 commanded by Lt-Col 'Rocky' Nelson. It was the third Marine attack squadron to re-equip with the Harrier, after VMA-513 and VMA-542. Still the overall experience level with the aircraft was very low, however.

'When I joined VMA-213 it had four pilots, we were just getting our act together. When the squadron got up to eight strong we went to Beaufort, South Carolina, where the first two Harrier squadrons were based. I was taught to fly the Harrier by pilots on VMA-542, some of whom had only 35 hours airborne in the type. They had been taught to fly it by the pilots of VMA-513, who had an average of about 50 hours on type after learning how to fly it with the Royal Air Force at Wittering. So it was a case of the blind leading the blind!

'After I had completed the ground school and learned the systems of the Harrier, Maj Tod Eikenbery briefed me for my first flight in the aircraft. This consisted of his asking "Have you got any questions?" I said "No." So he said "Let's go!" And that was the brief! At that time we had no two-seaters, so the first time we went out we were alone. I did a conventional take off and a conventional landing. The next flight was a conventional take off and a slow landing. It was not until my fifth flight in the Harrier that I did a vertical take off.

'In those days, when a pilot did his first vertical take-off, we used to invite the wives and girlfriends to see it. They would sit on blankets on the grass near the runway having lunch with the children, watching the pilots do their first hovers. It was wonderful fun.

'As I prepared for my first vertical take-off I remember thinking: "I've seen it done, I know it is scientifically possible, but it can't happen!" With the nozzles pointing down I slammed open the throttle, and the next thing I remember was my instructor saying on the radio "OK, ease power, ease power." By that time I was passing 200ft and still going up vertically!

'The Harrier turned out to be very easy to fly, a real pilot's airplane. It is not stable, it will not fly itself. Between 30 and 90kts [35 and 100mph] the Harrier is very unstable — it wants to swap ends all the time. But instability means manoeuvrability, and at speed it is so responsive. You are in charge. The airplane responds beautifully to control inputs. You can do rolls of 200-300deg per second. You can lay on $7\frac{1}{2}$g in half a second. In a dogfight, using vectored thrust, the bird

can really make your eyes water. At 450kts
[520mph] you can lay on $7\frac{1}{2}$g,
simultaneously pop the nozzles to the
braking stop, barrel roll and decelerate at up
to 50kts/sec. There is no aircraft in the world
that can stay with you doing that sort of
thing, not even another Harrier.'

Having an aircraft that is nice to fly is one
thing, having one that will effectively perform
the demanding ground attack mission is quite
another. Drax Williams has gone into detail
on the problem of providing rapid close air
support for the infantry in Vietnam using
conventional jet attack aircraft. How
different would things have been if the
Harrier had then been available?
'The Marine Corps bought the Harrier
because of its experience in Vietnam. Had we
had Harriers there, it would certainly have
made a big difference.

'The way our command and control
structure is set up in the Marine Corps is that
there is total flexibility. We have centralised
command but decentralised control.
Anybody in the field can raise his hand and
say "I need air support." And then somebody will make the decision to scramble
supporting aircraft, or divert an airborne aircraft from a lower priority target.

'Operating with the Harrier, the Marine Corps squadrons use three different types of bases. The largest, the main base, can be either an aircraft carrier or an airfield. That base has intermediate maintenance capability, navigation aids, all-weather approach aids, ammunition, fuel, ground support equipment, everything. Then, somewhat smaller and closer to the front line, is what we call a "facility" — an airstrip 600 to 800ft long and suitable for Harriers making short take-offs and landings (the Marine Corp's way of figuring out whether a strip of ground is flat enough for Harriers to make short take-offs, is to drive a jeep over it at 40mph; if the driver can stay in the vehicle, the strip is OK for the Harrier!). The facility will have squadron maintenance, basic navigational aids, fuel and ordnance. Then, smaller still and much closer to the front line, are the forward sites where the Harrier operates off hard ground, a strip of road, or a 72ft by 72ft pad of AM-2 [aluminium] matting or a plastic material we can spray on the ground.'

Since they are very easy to set up, a commander can have as many forward sites as he wishes each with one or more aircraft and providing either short or vertical take-offs and landings, depending on conditions.
'If we can make short take-offs from the forward site, we will. Hopefully we would be able to use a road or strip of flat ground. The best way to use a Harrier is with a short take off when it can get airborne with, typically, three 1,000lb and two 500lb bombs and full internal tanks with 5,200lb of fuel. Or it can carry more fuel for a greater endurance.

'If, on the other hand, it is possible at the forward sites to put down only small pads suitable for vertical take-offs and landings, the Harriers would use these. Taking off vertically the AV-8A Harrier cannot carry so much, say four 500lb bombs and 1,500 to 2,000lb of fuel in the internal tanks, sufficient for a 50-mile radius of action. But that is the worst case, and if you plan for the worst everything else is a little better than that.

'The idea is to have the Harrier fly from the facility to the forward site carrying its load of bombs. Then it lands and waits on the ground fairly close to the front line — within about 10 to 20 miles — with the pilot in the cockpit strapped in and ready to take-off at short notice, in radio contact with the forward air controller up with the infantry.'

The reader will note the differences between the Royal Air Force method of operating Harriers from dispersed sites, and those of the US Marines. In Germany the former would expect to have to support a defensive battle, in an area where a rapid advance by the enemy could overrun Harrier sites positioned too close to the front line; for this reason the Royal Air Force Harrier forward operating base is some 50 to 70 miles back from the front line, like the Marine 'facility'. The US Marine Harrier squadrons, on the other hand, would normally expect to be part of an amphibious landing force expanding a beachhead where there would be less risk of the forward site being overrun. It should be stressed, however, that either service could use either type of operating method if the combat situation required.

At the forward sites the Marine Harriers can receive virtually no support; normally there would be just one man there in addition to the pilot, to guide the aircraft down between any trees and assist it into a 'hide'.
'No ground support equipment is required to operate the Harrier from the forward site, not even chocks or steps. The Harrier sits on the ground waiting for the call for Close Air Support with the radio running off internal battery. The pilot watches the voltage indicator, and then the battery voltage starts to fall he starts the GTS [ground turbine start, a small gas turbine used for starting the main engine which also provides auxiliary electrical power]. This will re-charge the battery in about 10min, then the pilot has enough current for another $1\frac{1}{2}$ hours listening. The advantages of this type of operation over those by conventional attack aircraft are twofold: one, you can respond to requests for air support very quickly; and two, you're not burning gas in an airborne loiter — every gallon we don't burn is a gallon less we have to bring into the objective area.

'These forward sites will be close to friendly troops, for security. If the site itself comes under attack, at the first sign of the approach of enemy troops the Harrier can get airborne very quickly to deal with the threat, or escape from it.

'When a request for air support comes in, the Harriers can be airborne within a minute, and three or four minutes later they can be attacking targets. This could be happening at a dozen spots along the front line. Although airplanes might take off singly they will not normally attack alone; once in the air they will join up as pairs, or three- or four-ships.

'After a mission, if aircraft have suffered severe battle damage or require heavy maintenance work, the pilots will take them back to the main base. Otherwise the Harriers will return to the facility to refuel and rearm. And as soon as aircraft take off from their forward sites to go into action, others leave the facility to take their place.'

If appropriate, Harriers at the forward sites could be refuelled from transportable bladder tanks flown in by helicopter, and loaded with bombs by Marine infantrymen using the aptly nicknamed 'hernia bars'. But the forward sites would remain simple and austere, with an absolute minimum of provisions.

Drax Williams then described how the Marine Corps Harriers would be used to support an amphibious landing. The keynote of Harrier operations in this context is flexibility: the attack squadrons can operate against the enemy from the main base, the facility or the forward sites; of from all three simultaneously, as circumstances demand.

'The mission of the US Marine Corps is to mount amphibious landings on a hostile shore. So in any such action we would fly our first missions from a carrier or a remote base. Then, once the battle moves inland, a couple of lieutenants will go ashore, pick out the forward sites, and our engineers will spray plastic landing pads or put down AM-2 matting. Then we will fly in the first pair or three or six or however many Harriers are needed to provide the air support for the troops. As the battle moves further inland we will expand one of the forward sites into a facility, and a new set of forward sites will be established closer to the new battle line.

'As the front line advances further, a new facility might be established and then perhaps the old one made into a main base. And the whole time, the aircraft will be leapfrogging forward, staying as close as possible to the Marines in contact with the enemy in order to keep down the response time. So we are talking about 40 to 50 miles from the FEBA to a facility, and approximately 100 miles from the FEBA to the main base, but there can be total flexibility, the whole thing can be laid out as needed.

'For a while, every Marine battalion commander thought he was going to have a Harrier parked outside his command post to use as he wished. But the system doesn't

work like that, individual Harriers are not there to give direct support of anybody; they provide general support to troops in the area where and when it is needed. And besides, a Harrier parked outside a battalion command post would become a magnet for enemy mortar fire.

'This whole concept of facilities and forward sites would have worked very well in Vietnam. Da Nang and Chu Lai would have been the main bases. Phu Bai, Dong Ha, Khe Sanh and Cua Viet could have been facilities. The forward sites would have been wherever we needed them. The response time could have been 7 to 10min and 90% of the air control system bypassed.'

'Short sorties and lots of them'; that sums up the basic concept of Harrier close air support operations. But for this concept to work the aircraft really must be able to operate from forward sites with little or no maintenance support. All Marine Corps air squadrons have to undergo a Surge Sortie Test, to show they are able to fly a required sortie rate from their aircraft. For VMA-231 this moment of truth came on 7 December 1974.

'To see how well this particular forward site location would work, we landed two airplanes on Lyman Road, a standard 22ft wide

Harriers of VMA-542 pictured during operations embarked on the helicopter assault ship USS *Guam*. (*Above*) Harrier on the ship's starboard lift, with the pilot in the cockpit and the engine running prior to take-off.

Overleaf:
Left and top right: **Harrier deck landing sequence: hovering alongside the ship, moving across and landing on. (*Bottom right*) Harrier on the port lift, probably about to be lowered to the hangar deck.**

9
GUAM

9
GEEE
BEWARE OF JET BLAST
BEWARE OF ROTORS

country road which cuts through the middle of the Marine operating base at Camp Lejeune, North Carolina. It is a straight stretch of road about 1,500ft long, bordered on each side with pine trees. The Harriers did normal rolling landings at about 55kt [63mph] — the thin asphalt road is not strong enough to withstand the 21,000lb of thrust of a landing in the vertical mode, the surface would have broken up. After landing we turned off into a hide built amongst the trees with a floor of AM-2 matting; camouflage netting was strung across the top of the hide, so that the aircraft could not be seen from above.

'Then we started the test, against a target $7\frac{1}{2}$ miles away on Browns Island just off the coast. For each sortie the Harriers carried two 500lb bombs. We ran 42 sorties in 7hr, with an average sortie time of about 8min. The average turn-around time between sorties was about 12min. A pilot would fly six sorties, then another took his place. The airplanes just kept going. We had minor things go wrong, but the important things like the engine, the radio and the gunsight kept going.'

Although the Royal Air Force had conducted some trials operating Harriers from aircraft carriers, it was the US Marine Corps that deserves credit for developing the operational techniques of V/STOL at sea. The Marines quickly learned how effective their Harriers could be, operating from relatively small assault ships designed to carry helicopters.

'In the Mediterranean we had a friendly competition with the attack carrier USS *Constellation*, to see how rapidly we could launch aircraft. We were sailing side by side with *Connie*, and the word came "Go". We had nine Harriers lined up on deck, nose to tail, and they went off one every 10sec. We had nine launched in less than 90sec, and we were dropping 25lb practice bombs in the wake of *Connie* about eight miles away, before she had completed her turn into wind to launch her first aircraft . . .'

Harrier deck landings with a three-aircraft element were equally simple and rapid. On their return from sorties the three aircraft transitioned into the hover in line astern off the port side of the ship, then:

'The leader stops abeam the bow. No 2 stops amidships and No 3 stops abeam a point near the stern. As each aircraft comes into

55

position the LSO [landing signals officer] says "1, you're clear . . . 2 you're clear . . . 3 you're clear". And the Harriers slide across in turn and land. The only thing to avoid was having the No 2 or the No 3 land at the same time as the one in front, because if that happens the exhaust flows run back into the intakes of the aircraft behind and its engine loses power.

'We ended up being able to launch one aircraft every 10sec and recover one every 20sec, when operating multiple sorties.'

In May 1981, when he commanded VMA-542 as a Lieutenant-Colonel, Drax Williams took part in a full scale surge-sortie exercise with Harriers off the assault ship USS *Nassau* in the Mediterranean. During this exercise VMA-231 and VMA-542, each using six of the 10 Harriers each unit had embarked, flew a total of 72 sorties within 9hr: an average of six sorties per aircraft in use, throughout the day. The target was on the Tunisian coast near Bizerte, some 35 miles from the carrier, and three-aircraft Harrier elements attacked with practice bombs at 20min intervals all through the

daylight hours. Only one Harrier was unable to take-off as scheduled, and its place was taken by a standby aircraft. Drax Williams himself flew three of the 25min sorties, with a 55min turn-round between each.

'It was an overcast, foggy day and for a while we didn't know if we could run the exercise. But we decided to go ahead. We flew a very high rate of cyclic carrier operations. I remember going in at 250ft with my three Harriers at 510kt [590mph], and ahead I saw three small white clouds coming towards us at a tremendous speed, they were getting bigger very quickly. And at the front of the clouds were three dark noses — Harriers. It was Maj Joe Anderson of VMA-231 coming out with his three planes, the "clouds" were from the vapour condensation caused by the passage of the aircraft at high speed through the humid air. As we flashed by each other with a closing speed of over 1,000kt, we just quietly said "Hello" on the radio and disappeared in opposite directions.'

Although it is a subsonic attack aircraft, the Harrier soon demonstrated that in a dogfight it was no easy meat for supersonic fighters.

'In extremis, the Harrier can provide fighter cover for a beachhead. We think it is a very good point-defence fighter. All of our planes are fitted to carry Sidewinder, and we now have the AIM-9M version which is a very good missile.

'From the beginning we did a lot of simulated air-to-air combat in the Harrier. We fought against everything: the A-4, the F-4, the F-5, the A-6, the F-100, the F-105, F-106, the F-14, F-15 and F-16. When we started, the F-4 Phantom was the Marines' premier fighter. And when we engaged them in dogfights, they were literally murdered. They could knock us down from 18 miles in stand-off shots with Sparrows, there was nothing we could do about that. But in a dogfight it was different. We would pass each other and they would pull up into zoom climbs to about 35,000ft and then roll over on their backs to see where we were and decide what to do next. And almost every time there would be the little Harrier sitting at "dead six, in the saddle" [immediately behind, in a firing position] 1,200 ft away!

'In the climb the Harrier is superb. In March 1976 we ran a time-to-climb contest to 30,000ft, between a clean Harrier and a clean F-4. The Harrier beat the F-4 by 13sec.'

Having flown the Harrier in simulated dog fights with many other types of aircraft, was he surprised at the success of the Sea Harrier during the Falklands Conflict?

'I was totally convinced that if the Royal Navy pilots flew the airplane the way it should be flown, they were going to knock the hell out of the Argentine Air Force. I know what the Harrier can do. I have fought against A-4s in it and there is absolutely no way that an A-4 can knock down a Harrier — unless the A-4 is able to sneak in behind and the Harrier pilot doesn't see it coming. If the Harrier pilot sees it coming he can out-accelerate him, out-turn him, or zoom him. We fought hundreds of engagements against A-4s. The A-4 is a good airplane, but it is no match for a Harrier. I've never fought against a Mirage, but I suspect that unless it is a head-on pass at high altitude the weaponry was with the Royal Navy. At low altitude I am certain the Mirage cannot out-fight a Sea Harrier.'

Cdr Nigel 'Sharkey' Ward joined the Royal Navy in 1962 and, after gaining his watch-keeping ticket as a seaman officer in a frigate and minesweepers, began flying training for the Fleet Air Arm in 1966. Between 1969 and 1976 he completed two 2½-year operational tours flying Phantoms with No 892 Naval Air Squadron in HMS Ark Royal. *In 1976 he joined the Directorate of Naval Air Warfare at the Ministry of Defence in London, where he was responsible for many aspects of the Sea Harrier's development and introduction into service. Early in 1979 he was appointed Commanding Officer of the first Sea Harrier squadron, No 700A based at the Royal Naval Air Station Yeovilton, Somerset, which carried out the intensive flying trials with the new fighter. In 1981 he took command of No 801 Squadron in* HMS Invincible. *During the Falklands conflict he led the unit into action and flew more than 60 operational sorties in the Sea Harrier, in the course of which he shot down three enemy aircraft and became one of the top-scoring British pilots.*

The term 'flexibility of operations' is used so often to describe Sea Harrier deck operations that it has become a cliché; yet few people not closely connected with the aircraft have a full understanding of what the term means. In this section Nigel Ward draws on his uniquely comprehensive experience of both conventional and V/STOL carrier jet flying, to explain the significance of the Sea Harrier's 'flexibility of operation' when flying from a ship. In this account he concentrates on the landing, deck-handling and take-off aspects of deck operations; other operational aspects of flying the Sea Harrier will be covered in later chapters.

To give a yardstick for comparison, he begins with a description of the 'inflexibility of operation' of flying conventional jet fighters, Phantoms, from the 50,000 ton carrier HMS *Ark Royal*. Because landing such aircraft on a deck was so difficult, after they had converted to the Phantom ashore all new pilots had to undergo a course of highly specialised training before they could land on a carrier:

'Before going to a ship, a junior pilot had to practice the art of deck landing on an airfield painted with the markings of a carrier. He would do 50 or more practice deck landings using the deck landing projector sight, until he was assessed fully capable of landing on this very narrow runway at exactly the right speed, plus or minus 2kt, on exactly the right glide path.'

To land a conventional aircraft on a carrier safely, such accurate flying was essential:

'If the pilot was slightly out, with all the momentum of the aircraft at 140kt moving towards the ship, he might fail to catch an arrester wire, collide with one of the aircraft on the deck or hit the ramp at the back of the ship and kill himself. All of those things have been done.'

It was difficult enough to land a Phantom on a carrier by day; but by night the problems were compounded:

'In a conventional jet aircraft, a night carrier landing was considered 10 times more difficult than a daylight landing. At night all you could see on the approach was the projector sight, and a few lights to show the position of the deck. Imagine a darkened room with three very small pin-point lights on the wall, and stand 12yd away on the other side of the room with everything black around you. The three lights will subtend an angle of about 1deg from where you are looking. That was what the carrier looked like during an approach at night. When there was no horizon from moonlight, it was absolutely disorientating. You had to fly along an imaginary dotted line leading to the touch-down point and get everything right; it really was hard work.

'So considerable deck landing expertise was required for safe operations by conventional jet aircraft from a carrier. You acquired that only after a lot of training — which meant a lot of cost. Coast not only in terms of finance, but also cost in terms of flying time spent learning to land on a deck instead of learning other aspects of the aircraft's operational roles.'

During the take-off and landing of conventional aircraft, the carrier and her immediate escorts had to head into wind for several minutes, something they might not want to do in time of war.

'To launch or land conventional aircraft, the carrier had to point into wind. Now that was a constraint on the ship's operations, that she needed to turn into wind. A big ship takes a long time to alter direction, *Ark Royal* took about 3min to turn through 180deg. Not only did the carrier have to manoeuvre but also she need to stay protected, so the ships escorting her often had to manoeuvre too. Then there was the problem of what we call "restricted waterways", places where there are shallows or rocks, places you cannot take a big ship with a large turning circle. If the carrier was in restricted waters, sometimes she could not go in the direction she needed to in order to launch or recover her aircraft.

'Not only did the ship have to turn into wind, but if there was not enough natural wind she had to make her own by increasing speed. So the ship had to go where the aircraft needed her to. This took a lot of time

Below:
A glance at the competition: Sea Harrier XZ492 of No 800 Squadron, operating from HMS *Hermes*, pictured flying past the Soviet aircraft carrier *Minsk* with Ka-25 (NATO code-name 'Hormone') anti-submarine helicopters and Yak-36MP ('Forger') vertical take-off and landing fighters on her deck.

because in each launch/recovery cycle a carrier like *Ark Royal* would normally launch six Buccaneers and four Phantoms, then she had to recover a similar number of aircraft already airborne, after which the ship would turn out of wind and the deck could be prepared for the next launch.

'During intensive operations the deck was very busy receiving and dispatching aircraft, refuelling and rearming them, and moving the aircraft around so that all were in the correct order for the next launch. With conventional aircraft it was absolutely essential that the aircraft took off in the order required. This involved a lot of organisation and effort, and with flying in progress from *Ark Royal* the deck handling partly numbering dozens of men would be working flat out.'

Round-the-clock operations required two such shifts of deck handlers, comprising upwards of 50 men. Additionally, a similar number of men were needed to operate and maintain the steam catapults which launched the aircraft and the arrester gear which brought them to a halt. Carrier deck operations with conventional jet aircraft were (and in other navies still are) labour-intensive operations requiring considerable skill from all participants.

Deck launching and recovery operations by conventional jet aircraft were difficult enough when things went properly; but a relatively small hitch could bring everything to a grinding halt. Normally a conventional carrier would work to a $1\frac{1}{2}$hr launch and recovery cycle; at the end of each she would turn into wind, launch her ranged aircraft lined up on the deck, then those from the previous cycle would land on. The arrivals were refuelled and rearmed, the moved into position in the proper order for the next launch. Now consider what happened if one of the aircraft just launched had to return to the ship in difficulties, half an hour before the next launch was due:

'If we had an aircraft airborne which had an emergency and needed to land quickly or we would lose the aeroplane, we had to clear the deck runway so that he could land on the part with the arrester wires — and normally at this time it was covered in aircraft being prepared to launch. So we had to reorganise the whole deck in a panic, moving all of the aircraft on deck up to the bow or alongside the island, so that the aircraft in difficulty could land on But then we had to cancel the next launch, because we could not reposition the aircraft before the rest of the previous wave returned.'

In time of war it might be necessary to order the pilot of the aircraft returning with an emergency to bail out and lose the machine, rather than forgo an important launch (if, for example enemy aircraft have been detected about to attack the fleet). But, given the limited number of aircraft on a carrier, this would be an extremely difficult option for a commander to take.

Because of the problems likely to arise during deck operations with conventional aircraft, it was important that pilots did not allow their reserve fuel to fall below a certain minimum level; if they did, and something went wrong, there was a serious risk that aircraft would be lost because the tanks ran dry. In effect, this unusable fuel reserve was a millstone the aircraft had to carry throughout the entire sortie, to the detriment of its operating radius of action or its time on task. 'On the Phantom our peacetime minimum landing allowance was 2,500lb of fuel, enough for three good circuits and approaches to the deck. In the Phantom you could not predict how far that fuel would go because it took one mishap on deck, say a damaged or broken arrester wire from the previous land-on, and you would have to go round again while the damaged wire was cut out. That did not take long, but if aircraft were landing at 40sec intervals and you were waved off, you then started flying to conserve fuel until the deck handlers could sort out the problem (we could land at intervals of 25-30sec, but that left no margin for errors or hiccups; so if fuel was short people would go for the 40sec interval, because they could not risk having to go round again).'

So much for the difficulties of operating a force of 26 conventional jet aircraft, plus Gannet airborne early warning aircraft and helicopters, from the medium sized 50,000 ton *Ark Royal*. Now let us observe how much simpler it was to operate a similar number of Sea Harriers, Harriers and helicopters from the much smaller carrier *Hermes* (28,000 tons) during the Falklands Conflict. The V/STOL aircraft were able to make vertical landings on any spot on the deck that was clear, regardless of what was going on elsewhere on the deck and regardless of the ship's speed or its heading with respect to the wind; so an aircraft returning early usually landed with no drama of any sort. Take-offs could be made when the ship was heading into wind, downwind or even across-wind up to reasonable limits.

There is no need for the pilots of V/STOL aircraft to undergo a lengthy and highly specialised training in deck operations: a vertical landing on to a ship is not all that different from a vertical landing on to a pad ashore. This was demonstrated in most convincing fashion by the Harrier pilots of No 1 Squadron, Royal Air Force, none of whom had experience of carrier V/STOL operations before the Falklands Conflict. To prepare him for the new role, each pilot made a couple of practice ski-jump take-offs at Yeovilton to assure himself that the operation was as easy as everyone had said it was; then they flew their aircraft to Ascension Island, and after a short stop landed them on the deck of the container ship *Atlantic Conveyor*. The Harriers sailed to the South Atlantic parked on the ship's deck, and 11 days later lifted off vertically and flew over to *Hermes* which was cruising nearby. Once on the carrier the RAF pilots had *one day* to familiarise themselves with deck operations, and on the next they flew their first attack mission against the enemy. During the four weeks that followed the normally shore-based No 1 Squadron flew 126 tasked sorties against the enemy, in the course of which there was only one minor deck landing mishap (accident is too strong a word) in which the aircraft suffered no damage. These operations show clearly the huge difference V/STOL has brought to deck-landing opera-

tions; certainly no shore-based squadron flying conventional jet aircraft would have attempted to operate from a carrier with so little training.

With the Harrier or Sea Harrier, every aspect of deck operations is much easier than with conventional jet aircraft:

'The Sea Harrier can taxi backwards under its own power. You don't need to put a tractor on it. You can start it up wherever it is on the deck; if you are pointing against a bulkhead, you put the nozzles forward and back-taxi out of that spot, then put the nozzles aft and taxi around the deck. It is so very simple. Compared with the large number of handlers we needed to move the aircraft around the deck of *Ark Royal*, on that of *Invincible* we do the same thing with five men. We still use a tractor to tow Sea Harriers if we want to move them and there is no pilot available, but there is much less of this than there used to be.

'With the Sea Harrier it is not so important to lay out the deck so aircraft can take off in a required order. On the deck of *Hermes*, for example, where there is more space than that of *Invincible*, there was hardly any need to do it at all. There is a serried rank of aircraft along the port side, and anyone can pull out and take off whenever he needs to. You can almost do the same from *Invincible*, but not with quite the same degree of flexibility.'

As well as requiring far fewer men to position the aircraft on the deck for V/STOL operations, the ship itself needs no catapult or arrester gear nor specialised crewmen to operate and maintain them; it all means that, for V/STOL operations of a given number of aircraft, a far smaller and cheaper ship can be used.

The 'dead weight' of the fuel reserve that has to be carried around during a Sea Harrier mission is considerably smaller than that for conventional jet aircraft. As a result, the V/STOL aircraft is able to operate much closer to its brochure performance than can conventional naval aircraft:

'In the Phantom we would use 1,500lb of fuel for the start-up, launch and acceleration to climbing speed. That is a lot. In the Sea Harrier, doing the same thing we use less than 400lb. The Sea Harrier does not use a lot of fuel to get airborne, and it does not use that much to land. And because you can predict exactly when you are going to land, or land when you need to, you can land with very low margins of fuel. Everybody who builds an aircraft brings out a glossy brochure giving the performance details but these omit things like the fuel reserves necessary for safe operations. The brochures for the Harrier, Sea Harrier and AV-8A are good because they do not exaggerate. I believe the US Marine Corps say the AV-8A is the only aircraft they have that has been able to do everything the brochure says it can.

'The term "have to go round again" is virtually unknown for the Sea Harrier. Only if something dreadful goes wrong, particularly at night, might such an occasion arise. In peacetime we try to be in the hover for landing with a minimum of 800lb of fuel

by day, and about 1,200lb at night so there is fuel to go round again if necessary.

'In war, I never got back to the ship with more than 500lb of fuel, and I flew more than 60 sorties by day and night. When I returned after shooting down the C-130 [on 1 June 1982] I was very low on fuel, I had about 150lb left — enough for about four minutes cruising flight with the aircraft "clean", two minutes with the gear and flaps down or about a minute in the hover. I was short of fuel but I was not desperate as I was able to calculate on the computer the exact amount of fuel required for what I was going to do. On the way back to *Invincible* the assault ships *Fearless* and *Intrepid* in San Carlos Water offered us their decks in case we needed to make emergency landings. I asked my wing man, Steve Thomas, "How is your fuel, are you going to make it?" I told him I intended to go back to *Invincible* rather than to land on the assault ships. I knew I could get back. He said "It's all right Boss, I'll get back too". We could see the ship from 60 miles that day, and our fuel worked out exactly as we had predicted. You can predict fuel consumption very accurately in the Sea Harrier. I knew that if I could get back to the ship with a certain amount of fuel, it did not matter what was going on on deck, I could put the aircraft down. With the Sea Harrier you pick your spot on the deck, then land on just like a helicopter.

'With the Sea Harrier there is no over-riding need for an interval between aircraft coming in to land; if a division of aircraft returns short of fuel they can land successively on different parts of the deck. There is no need to get the tidy landing sequence going. Only if there had been a dis-aster like a crash on the deck would aircraft *need* to land on the same spot. The fastest we ever had four Sea Harriers land on the same spot was 48sec, from the time the first one touched down to the time the fourth touched.'

Although a night deck landing in a Sea Harrier is more difficult than one by day, the operation is still considerably easier and safer than with a conventional jet aircraft:
'You aim not for a point, but for an envelope in the sky where you can decelerate into the hover before landing-on. As you decelerate into the hover it does not matter exactly where you stop, within reason, because you can adjust your position in the hover before you land. So you do not need the precise posi-tioning that is necessary with a conventional aircraft.

'Now we have a projector sight landing system to assist us during landing on, we can operate at night almost at will. Most of our new pilots fly the Sea Harrier off and land on to the deck at night during their first tour, which was unusual with conventional jet air-craft (the US Navy pilots do it, but they have much bigger carriers from which to operate).'

Many of the 'party tricks' used by the Harrier during air displays, like being able to stop and hover, fly backwards or sideways, make a fundamental difference to its value as a carrier-borne fighter:
'The ability to do such things, to be able to go backwards or hover while one decides what to do, has saved the situation for me on two occasions. For example, during a work-up with one of the carriers, a helicopter flew across my nose as I was on the final approach to land. He realised what he was doing, but backed away from me towards the ship across the line that I was taking. Had I been in a conventional jet either I would have gone into the water, or there would have been a collision and we both would have gone into the water. But I pushed my nozzles forward to slow down fast, and went low and to the left of him. I ended up in the hover a quarter of a mile from the ship's beam, at about 30ft, thinking "Thank goodness that worked out all right!" Then I just translated sideways to the ship and landed. End of problem.

'The Sea Harrier's versatility has pre-vented many such incidents developing into

Below:
Lt-Cdr Robin Kent of No 800 Squadron making the first landing in a Royal Navy Sea Harrier on the deck of HMS *Invincible* during her initial work-up in the summer of 1980. Nigel Ward was flying the second aircraft, awaiting its turn.

Above:
XZ438, first of the three pre-production Sea Harriers, pictured carrying dummy Sea Eagle long range anti-shipping missiles; (*Top right*) **XZ440, the third pre-production Sea Harrier, taking off from the ski jump at Bedford carrying two dummy Sea Eagles and two dummy Sidewinder air-to-air missiles;** (*Bottom right*) **XZ440 releasing a Sea Eagle during an early trial, with a centre-mounted camera pod to photograph the results.**

accidents, and has saved several aircraft. That knowledge helps give the pilot peace of mind. When you are put into a spot in this aircraft, you usually have many options on how you get out of it. And if all else fails you can stop, assess the position and then do something about it.'

The ski-jump, the raised bow fitted to modern Royal Navy carriers, has added to the ease and safety of Sea Harrier deck operations by ensuring that at take-off the aircraft leaves the deck heading upwards and away from the surface of the sea:

'Taking off from a flat deck in the Sea Harrier, as you reached the end of the deck you had to make sure you put your nozzles down, from pushing you forwards to half pushing you upwards as well. My senior pilot on 700A Squadron, Lt-Cdr Tony Ogilvy, used to say to himself as he accelerated towards the end of the deck: "Metal, metal, metal, water, nozzles . . .". But the flat deck did not point upwards, or throw you up into the sky. So if things went wrong there was not much time to react: during a take off from a flat deck, in a Sea Harrier or a conventional aircraft, if something goes seriously wrong the average time between leaving the

deck and impacting with the sea is something like three seconds.

'The ski-jump gives you the same cue that you get when you go over a hump-backed bridge. The G comes on, and when it goes off you know you are off the ski-jump. Then you put your nozzles down to the pre-selected setting, and you are then going skywards quite fast with all the time in the world if anything goes wrong — the machine just cannot go straight back down into the water. It is going up and so even if you have a catastrophic problem you have at least 8sec to sort your aircraft out, perhaps jettisoning underwing stores, or get out. Eight seconds is like an hour when you are thinking as fast as you are when you are getting airborne. So the ski-jump is a very safe way of getting airborne. It is also the easiest way of launching a Sea Harrier, by day or night; and, as an added bonus, for a given take-off run the aircraft can carry a fuel/weapons load about a quarter greater when flying off the ski-jump compared with a flat deck.'

In considering the usefulness of V/STOL to deck operations by jet fighters, the most important question is: does it make the aircraft more effective in time of war? The answer, based on the experience of the Falklands Conflict, is a clear and resounding 'Yes'.

Deck operations by conventional jet aircraft from medium-sized or small carriers are always difficult. And with a little interference from the weather they become impossible. During the Falklands Conflict the 20,000 ton Argentine carrier *25 de Mayo* attempted to launch an air strike against the British task force with her Skyhawk attack aircraft just before dawn on 2 May 1982. But when she reached her flying-off position there was insufficient wind for her aircraft to take off carrying bombs, and she had to abandon the attempt. These same calm conditions imposed no hindrance on jet operations from the British carriers, however, and on occasions Sea Harriers were launched even when there was a relative *tail* wind across the deck; the limiting maximum wind speed for launches was that at which the deck crews could work without serious risk of being blown overboard (beyond that, if there was an absolute operational need to launch Sea Harriers, the men would have to wear lifelines). Sea Harriers were launched regardless of how badly the ship's deck was pitching; and they could land-on under the same conditions, using the old helicopter trick of setting down amidships at the point about which the carrier's motion pivots and vertical movement is at a minimum. During the conflict operational requirements sometimes dictated that Sea Harriers were air borne when the weather suddenly deteriorated. On the night of 5 June 1982, for example, Lt Charles Cantan of No 801 Squadron was airborne when a dense fog descended around the British ships. He approached *Invincible* using radar, decelerated to the hover at 200ft instead of the normal 70ft, then continued slowly towards the carrier until he saw the beam from her searchlight shining vertically upwards. He descended through the gloom following the beam, and landed on the deck with a horizontal visibility less than 50yd.

It has to be admitted that some of the things that the Sea Harrier does can be done better by conventional jet aircraft operating from the US Navy's 90,000 ton super-carriers. With their powerful three-stage catapults, these ships can launch aircraft regardless of the wind speed. And it takes an extraordinarily rough sea before the pitching of the deck makes landing impossible by day or night. With their air groups of more than

90 high-performance aircraft, these ships are by far the most powerful warships afloat. This type of vessel is the 'Rolls-Royce' answer to the problem of providing and exploiting air power at sea; and, like the Rolls Royce car, just about the *only* thing to be said against them is the expense of buying and maintaining such a piece of machinery. At 1980s prices a 90,000 ton super-carrier costs about $1.5billion, without aircraft. This puts such vessels beyond the reach of all but the most wealthy navies; at the time of writing only the US Navy possesses such ships. And even a super-carrier cannot recover aircraft when it is not heading into wind, nor would it attempt to do so in the visibility conditions in which Charles Cantan landed his Sea Harrier on the 19,500 ton HMS *Invincible*.

For jet fighter operations from medium-sized or small carriers, which is what the majority of navies have to use if they are to project air power at sea, the Sea Harrier offers by far the most cost-effective solution in terms of the number of effective war sorties possible per day, for a given financial expenditure. Gradually, the world's navies are coming to realise that V/STOL has indeed added a new dimension to deck operations.

Flt Lt Dave Morgan joined the Royal Air Force in 1969 and his first operational tour was with a Wessex helicopter squadron. In 1977 he converted on to the Harrier GR3 and flew it with No 3 Squadron in Germany, amassing over 800 hours on this type. In February 1982 he was seconded to the Fleet Air Arm and joined No 899 Squadron, the Sea Harrier conversion unit at Yeovilton in Somerset, to begin training.

When the Falklands crisis erupted he had not completed the Sea Harrier course, but was sent to join No 800 Squadron on Hermes. *During the conflict he flew 50 operational sorties and caused the destruction of two Skyhawks and a Puma helicopter in the air, and probably an Islander light transport on the ground. In addition he shared in the destruction of two helicopters, a Puma and an Agusta 109, with other pilots. This made him the top-scoring British pilot during the conflict, and afterwards he was awarded the Distinguished Service Cross.*

For Dave Morgan the Falklands Crisis broke at 8am on Friday 1 April, the morning the Argentine troops landed on the Falklands.
'I came in at 8am as on a normal morning, having heard of the invasion on the BBC, to find everyone else already in the crewroom. I walked in and said "Have you heard, the Argies are having a go at the Falklands!" Back came the chorus "What do you think we've been doing here for the last few hours!" They had been called in at about 4am, but because I was a trainee I had not been on the recall list.

'People were rushing around preparing aircraft. Because I had completed only two-thirds of the course, the initial thought was

that I should stay at Yeovilton to finish the course. Later in the day it was decided that I was to go down to the South Atlantic as an operations officer. And later still it was decided to send south every possible Sea Harrier pilot immediately available, including a naval guy on the course with me with only about 80 hours on type.'

At the time *Hermes* and *Invincible* were both in harbour and their Sea Harrier squadrons, Nos 800 and 801 respectively, were disembarked at Yeovilton. The aircraft and pilots of No 899 Squadron were divided between the two operational squadrons, and Dave Morgan was allocated to No 800 Squadron. He made his first-ever deck landing the following day, on *Hermes* as she lay alongside the harbour at Portsmouth loading stores. The aircraft he brought was XZ450, the first production Sea Harrier, which had been engaged in trials with the Sea Eagle anti-ship missile and still carried the fittings for this weapon.

On the way south the Sea Harrier pilots went into intensive training for the tasks they would carry out in action. The aircraft's primary role was to provide air defence for the fleet, its secondary role was anti-shipping strike and its tertiary role was reconnaissance. To this was now added a new role, that of attacking ground targets.

The first encounter between a Sea Harrier and an Argentine aircraft occurred on 21 April, and came as a surprise to both sides:
'We were intercepting anything that came within range. It was just a standard intercept on what we thought was a civil airliner. Lt Simon Hargreaves from 800 Squadron closed in and saw it was a Boeing 707, then said he was going to take a closer look. He was surprised to see that the aircraft carried Argentine Air Force markings. At the time we were not cleared to engage or harass their aircraft, so he could only take photographs.'

During the days that followed the Sea Harriers received clearance first to harass the Argentine aircraft that came near the Task Force, then later they received orders to shoot them down. But before these orders could be enacted the Argentine Air Force stopped sending its Boeings in the vicinity of the British carriers.

On 30 April, following the failure to find a diplomatic solution to the crisis acceptable to both sides, the British Task Force received orders to begin operations aimed at removing the Argentine forces from the Falkland Islands. The initial operations were to begin with an attack on Port Stanley airfield by a single Vulcan bomber from Ascension Island, during the early morning darkness on 1 May. Four hours later, after dawn, 12 Sea Harriers from *Hermes* were to attack the airfields at Port Stanley and Goose Green. *Invincible's* Sea Harriers were to provide top cover in case Argentine fighters attempted to interfere with the operation.

With three other pilots who had previous ground-attack experience with the Royal Air Force, Flt Lts Ted Ball and Tony Penfold, and Lt Clive Morell, Dave Morgan planned a co-ordinated attack on Port Stanley airfield to be made by nine of the available Sea Harriers. The attack was to open with four toss-bombing aircraft running in from the north-east; three of them were to release 1,000lb bombs with VT (radar airburst) fuses, aimed to explode over the anti-aircraft gun positions on Mary Hill and Canopus Hill to the northwest and southwest of the airfield, and the fourth aircraft was to attack with 1,000 pounders fitted with a mixture of instantaneous and delayed action fuses. While the defenders were thus distracted the other five Sea Harriers, the lay-down bombers, were to attack the airfield with cluster bombs and parachute retarded 1,000 pounders. The remaining three Sea Harriers were to go to Goose Green, and deliver a straight in attack on the airfield there. Dave

Below:
A Sea Harrier of No 800 Squadron moving in to land on the deck of *Hermes*. The photograph was taken from the island on the starboard side of the carrier, indicating that the aircraft was landing with its nose pointing into the relative wind which was coming over the ship's stern This method is common for the Sea Harrier, but impossible for conventional naval fixed winged aircraft.

At the time of the launch *Hermes* was about 100 miles east-north-east of Port Stanley. Dave Morgan took off second, after Lt-Cdr Andy Auld who was leading the mission.

'We took off at first light, it was light enough to fly visually, but dark enough for us to need to put on our anti-collision lights for the join up. Once we had assembled in formation everyone switched off his lights, we descended to 50ft and headed to a point to the north of East Falkland. It was a grey day, and I remember seeing the north coast of the island, Macbride Head, coming out of the mist. As we came in over the Head the five of us in the lay-down aircraft turned left into a 360deg holding pattern, to give the correct separation from the toss bombers at the target. I watched the toss bombers heading away from us, to the southeast.'

After completing his turn Dave Morgan headed towards the target, hugging the undulating ground.

'I did not see the VT fused bombs go off. The first thing I saw, as I came over the ridge by Mount Low, was a lot of explosions over the top of the airfield at about 200ft. I thought "Christ, the cluster bombs are going off early!" They were not supposed to go off before they hit the ground. But in fact it was not the cluster bombs, it was anti-aircraft fire aimed at the aircraft ahead of me. As I crossed over Port Stanley harbour at 50ft my radar warning receiver picked up the signals from a Fledermaus fire control radar on search. So I eased down the nose and went lower. All I could see in front of me were the tops of the sand dunes. From two or three places there were twinkling lights; I didn't see any tracer, but obviously there were guys there firing at me.

'As I passed over the sand dunes I pulled up to about 150ft getting ready to drop my load of cluster bombs, then I saw some of the damage done to the airfield. One of the buildings was covered in flames, with billowing black smoke coming out of the back. There was lots of anti-aircraft fire, and missiles going all over the place. A Tigercat missile came along the runway and passed in front of my nose, probably aimed at Tony Penfold who attacked ahead of me.'

Dave Morgan aimed his cluster bombs at the Islander light transport aircraft which had previously belonged to the British governor of the Falklands, and which had been captured by the Argentine forces. This air-

Morgan was to fly as one of the lay-down bombers attacking Port Stanley airfield.

'We were not very keen on going in after the Vulcan, we wanted to be first in. We were a bit concerned that the Vulcan attack had woken them up, and we would be putting our heads into a hornets' nest. And it also gave them time to get Mirages over from the mainland if they wanted to.

'We knew that we would get a lot of AA fire and missiles over the target, and that worried us. For me the Roland missiles were the big worry. But I had looked at its parameters and I thought that so long as we stayed ultra low they would not get us.

'As we came out on the deck of *Hermes* there were the aircraft lined up, with their bombs on. As many aircraft as possible were lined up on the centreline, the rest were in herringbone pattern facing aft. It was a peculiar feeling, the adrenalin was pumping around like mad. Everybody was very quiet, people were not saying a great deal. There were a few half-hearted jokes and a few nervous titters around the place. Everyone was fairly withdrawn.'

craft had its tail blown off during the attack and Dave Morgan 'claims responsibility' for its destruction. While in the bombing run his Sea Harrier was hit by anti-aircraft fire.

'Suddenly there was a bloody great explosion behind me and the rudder started vibrating like mad. At the time I was hit I was going pretty fast, 500-600kt [630-690mph], with the throttle hard forward. The aircraft was still responding to the controls; I took a quick look inside the cockpit to see if the engine instruments looked all right. They did.

'As I eased the aircraft back to ground level through the smoke a Fledermaus radar locked on to me, so I blipped open my air-brake to dump chaff and pulled round hard to the left. That broke the lock-on and I continued round until I was heading east back to the ship.

'Once out of range of the defences I began climbing to altitude to return to the carrier, I slowed down and the vibration decreased markedly. Now I had time to look around, and it was clear there was a failure of the electrical rudder trimming system. That seemed to confirm that the hit had been on or

This page:
Pre-flight checks of aircraft No 27 (XZ 496) of No 800 Squadron on *Hermes*. While flying this aircraft on the afternoon of 21 May 1982, Lt-Cdr Mike Blissett (*Below*) shot down a Skyhawk of Grupo 4.

Facing page, top :
Armourers on HMS *Hermes* loading an AIM-9L Sidewinder missile on a Sea Harrier of No 800 Squadron. This type of missile destroyed 18 Argentine aircraft during the Falklands conflict and contributed to the destruction of one more, reportedly for an expenditure of 26 missiles. Although this weapon has been credited with an all-aspect homing capability, during the operations in the South Atlantic all of the missiles which destroyed aircraft were fired from the rear hemisphere.

Facing page, bottom:
HMS *Hermes* in the South Atlantic, passing fuel to the frigate HMS *Broadsword*. Even though at the time of the photograph the carrier was steaming downwind at moderate speed with both lifts down, in this condition she could still have launched and recovered Sea Harriers and Harriers; this is the degree of flexibility the V/STOL jets have brought to shipborne operations. *MoD*

near the rudder. But I made another check to confirm that there were no problems with the engine or any fuel leaks.'

On the way back to the carrier Flt Lt Ted Ball moved into formation on the damaged Sea Harrier to look it over.
'He came up on the port side and said he couldn't see any damage. He asked me to move the rudder pedals, and said he could see the rudder moving OK. Then he went around to the starboard side and said "Ah, yes, you've got a hole in the fin."'
'*Hermes* picked us up on radar and guided us back, then I orbited the carrier while everyone else landed. Then they cleared the deck, parked all the other aircraft down one side. While that was happening I did a low speed handling check; I reduced speed to 120kt [138mph], and everything seemed all right: the nozzles were working, there was duct pressure. When the deck was clear I slowed down gently and landed, running in at 20 to 30kt to make a rolling vertical landing. I didn't want to make a vertical landing in case I heated up the ducts and they seized. Once on the deck, I rolled to a stop near the bow and shut down.'

He climbed out of his aircraft and strode round to the tail to join the knot of people surveying the damage. An anti-aircraft shell, almost certainly a 20mm, had made a hole about the size of a 10-pence piece on the port side of the fin, then exploded and blown a hole the size of a man's fist on the starboard side. Within a few hours the Sea Harrier was repaired and ready for action again. One of the sailors saved the circle of metal cut from around the hole, carefully mounted it on a wooden plaque and later presented it to the pilot as a memento of the occasion.

During the days that followed Dave Morgan had no further encounter with the enemy until 9 May, when he and Lt-Cdr Gordon Batt took off at dawn for a high altitude attack on Port Stanley runway. Following the loss of Lt Nick Taylor's Sea Harrier to anti-aircraft fire at Goose Green on 4 May, these aircraft were restricted to bombing attacks which did not take them within effective range of the enemy gun and missile defences. Such high altitude attacks lacked accuracy, however, and stood little chance of securing a hit on the runway.

'We were going in to bomb Port Stanley airfield at 18,000ft. At this stage we were

harassing the guys there, we would go over and loose off our bombs at the runway. But we had been briefed not to bomb if the airfield was covered in cloud: we wanted to be absolutely certain we did not hit Stanley town and cause casualties amongst the Falklanders.

'When we arrived we found the airfield completely covered in cloud. So we were told to fly a combat air patrol, controlled by HMS *Coventry*. As I turned away from Stanley at 18,000ft I switched on my radar and about 60 miles south east of Stanley, well inside the Total Exclusion Zone, I saw a ship on my radar. I reported this to *Coventry* and asked if it was one of ours. They said it wasn't, and asked us to investigate. We headed towards the radar contact, descended through cloud and emerged at 500ft. As we closed on the ship it proved to be a large stern trawler, heading west.'

As the two Sea Harriers flew past the vessel, Batt observed that she was flying the Argentine flag. Dave Morgan climbed to report this to *Coventry*, and while he was doing so Batt made another run past and read the ship's name: *Narwal*. Dave Morgan reported all of this to the control ship.
'*Coventry* told us to stand by. Then a couple of minutes later came the order "Engage it". I passed the message to Gordie who said "OK, I'll give her a quick shot over the bow first". He fired across her bow, but she kept going west. We were still carrying our 1,000lb bombs which we would have to drop into the sea, as we could not land on the carrier with them still on. They were rigged for high level attack, with a 7sec arming delay between release and then they became "live". That meant they would not be armed in time if we released them at low level, but we thought we might as well aim them at an Argentine ship as anywhere else. I made my attack and the bomb just missed her funnel and went into the sea beside her. Then Gordie came in from the other side and his bomb struck the ship on the port side near the bow. But, as expected, it was still "safe" and failed to explode.'

Following this the two Sea Harriers each made three strafing attacks on the ship during which they scored numerous hits. Her engine room badly damaged, *Narwal* slid to a stop and began to drift. Later a Sea King helicopter landed a Royal Navy boarding party on the ship; one of the crew taken prisoner was an Argentine naval officer, and captured documents indicated that the ship had been involved in intelligence gathering. Although attempts were made to save her as a prize, *Narwal* sank the next day.

Like other Sea Harrier pilots Dave Morgan was worked hard on 21 May, the day of the British landings at around San Carlos Water.

Above:
A Skyhawk of Grupo 5 of the Argentine Air Force on its way to the Falklands taking on fuel from a KC–130 tanker, with another pair in the background doing the same thing. On the afternoon on 8 June 1982 Dave Morgan shot down two Skyhawks of Grupo 5 near Bluff Cove; Lt Dave Smith, flying ao Morgan'o wing man, shot down a third. *via Ethell*

'For every mission, we would spend about four hours on standby. At any one time *Hermes* would have two aircraft on combat air patrol, two on their way out to relieve them and two on their way back from the patrol area. One of the patrol lines was to the north of Falkland Sound, to the north of Goat Hill, a second was near Clay Mount on West Falkland and a third was over Swan Island. The altitude of the combat air patrols depended on the amount of cloud and its base: you wanted to fly as high as possible to conserve fuel, but you had to be able to see enemy aircraft running in at low altitude.

'Once or twice I was vectored towards incoming contacts, but I never got a sniff of any of their fighter-bombers during the "Bomb Alley" battle.'

Dave Morgan's next contact with the enemy was on the morning of the 23rd, when he was flying a combat air patrol over Falkland Sound with another Royal Air Force Sea Harrier pilot, Flt Lt John Leeming. Suddenly the two pilots had an opportunity to deplete further the limited Argentine helicopter lifting capacity on the islands.

'We were on patrol over Swan Island at 8,000ft, keeping watch on one of the routes used by their fighter-bombers. As I was turning over Shag Cove, I caught sight of a low flying helicopter heading north over the cove. Its pilot had made a serious error. If there is one thing you learn when doing knap-of-the-earth helicopter flying, that is to avoid passing over water features if you can possibly avoid it. If you do go over them, you can be seen for miles. At the time I didn't know if it was one of our's, so I asked the controlling ship. He said "Hang on, I'll find out." We were low on fuel and didn't have time to hang on, so John and I dropped down to investigate. The helicopter was at about 150ft, I ran in at him head-on. And at about 500yd I recognised it as a Puma — and we did not have any Pumas on the Falklands. I called it as "Hostile" to John, and he replied, "Hey, there's four of them!" Then I made out two more Pumas following the first and an Agusta 109 on the end. I went straight for the leading Puma but it was too late to engage; I turned over the top of him and was pulling up to get into a firing position, when out of the corner of my eye I saw the Puma I had flown over smash into the ground and explode in a ball of fire."

Neither pilot had fired at the Puma: either the slipstream from Dave Morgan's aircraft had caught it and sent it out of control, or the pilot had lost control trying to evade. On examination after the war the Puma was found to have been heavily laden with mortar bombs, so there would have been little reserve performance in hand. The two RAF pilots had no time to ponder the matter, however, for there were other important targets in the area waiting to be hit. The

Agusta 109 was either on the ground with the rotor turning, or in a low hover. Leeming stafed it first, then Dave Morgan ran to attack.

'I ran in and put a lot of rounds in the area around him, I saw at least one solid hit; there was a large fuel explosion and the helicopter began to burn. We were just about to depart the area when John said "There's another Puma shut down further up the valley!" The crew had obviously plonked the helicopter down on the valley floor and run away. I fired the remainder of my rounds at it, then my guns emptied. I didn't hang around to see if I had done any damage.'

As he climbed away he reported the position of the helicopter to the control ship, and soon afterwards a pair of Sea Harriers from No 801 Squadron arrived and finished it off.

Following the heavy air attacks on British ships engaged in or covering the landings at San Carlos, on 21, 23, 24 and 25 May, there were two weeks with little Argentine air activity over the Falklands. This period of calm came to an abrupt halt early on the afternoon of 8 June, with the devastating attack on the landing ships *Sir Galahad* and *Sir Tristram* off Fitzroy by Skyhawks of Grupo 5. Too late, the Sea Harriers were sent to mount a standing patrol over the area.

'I was with Lt Dave Smith, we were briefed to fly a combat air patrol south of Bluff Cove. We heard that the landing ships had been hit and were scrambled shortly after that. We had been programmed to fly at about that time, because Dave and I needed night landings to complete our night deck qualification. The idea was that we would take off in daylight and land after dark.

'We arrived over Bluff Cove and relieved a couple of 801 Squadron guys who had been on patrol at 10,000ft. There was a lot of smoke rising from the burning ships off Fitzroy, you could see it 40 miles away.

'We began our patrol, and below us I saw a landing craft gently trogging along the coast. I asked the control ship whether it was friendly, and they said it was. By that time we had about two minutes' fuel left before we had to go back to the carrier, and were doing a final turn from east back on to the west.

'I glanced back at the landing craft and saw an aircraft low down going straight for it, about 300yd away. Beforehand I had briefed Dave that whoever saw an enemy aircraft first was to dive after it, and the other guy would tag along. That was exactly what happened.

'I pushed my throttle forward, rolled over on my back and went down after him. Dave followed me. In the dive I noticed there were two more aircraft following the first. One got a bomb on the back end of the landing craft and it went off with a large explosion; that made me very angry. When I was down to about 2,000ft I saw a fourth aircraft trailing the rest. I decided to go for him.'

In the half-light Dave Morgan thought the enemy aircraft were Mirages, but in fact they were Skyhawks from Grupo 5 — the same unit that had carried out the attack on the landing ships earlier in the day. Now the two British pilots were about to extract revenge.

'I wound across and got in behind with a massive overtaking speed. He was rapidly getting larger in my windscreen. I locked up my missile at about 1,500yd and fired at 1,000yd. My missile did a quick initial jink, then went off after him and exploded near his tail; there was a huge fireball and wreckage began to fall into the water. There was no reaction at all from the others, they were in a gaggle coming off the target with no attempt at mutual cover. They were running west up Choiseul Sound.

'I then pulled across after one of the others, who had seen either me or the explosion. He began a fairly gentle turn to port across my nose, almost as if he was looking to see what had happened to the man behind. My missile locked up, broke lock, then I locked it on again and this time the lock held. I fired at the second aircraft at about 1,200yd. I think he saw it coming, because he reversed his turn and broke away to starboard. The missile reversed its turn too, cut across my nose and went straight in and hit after he had turned through about 40deg.

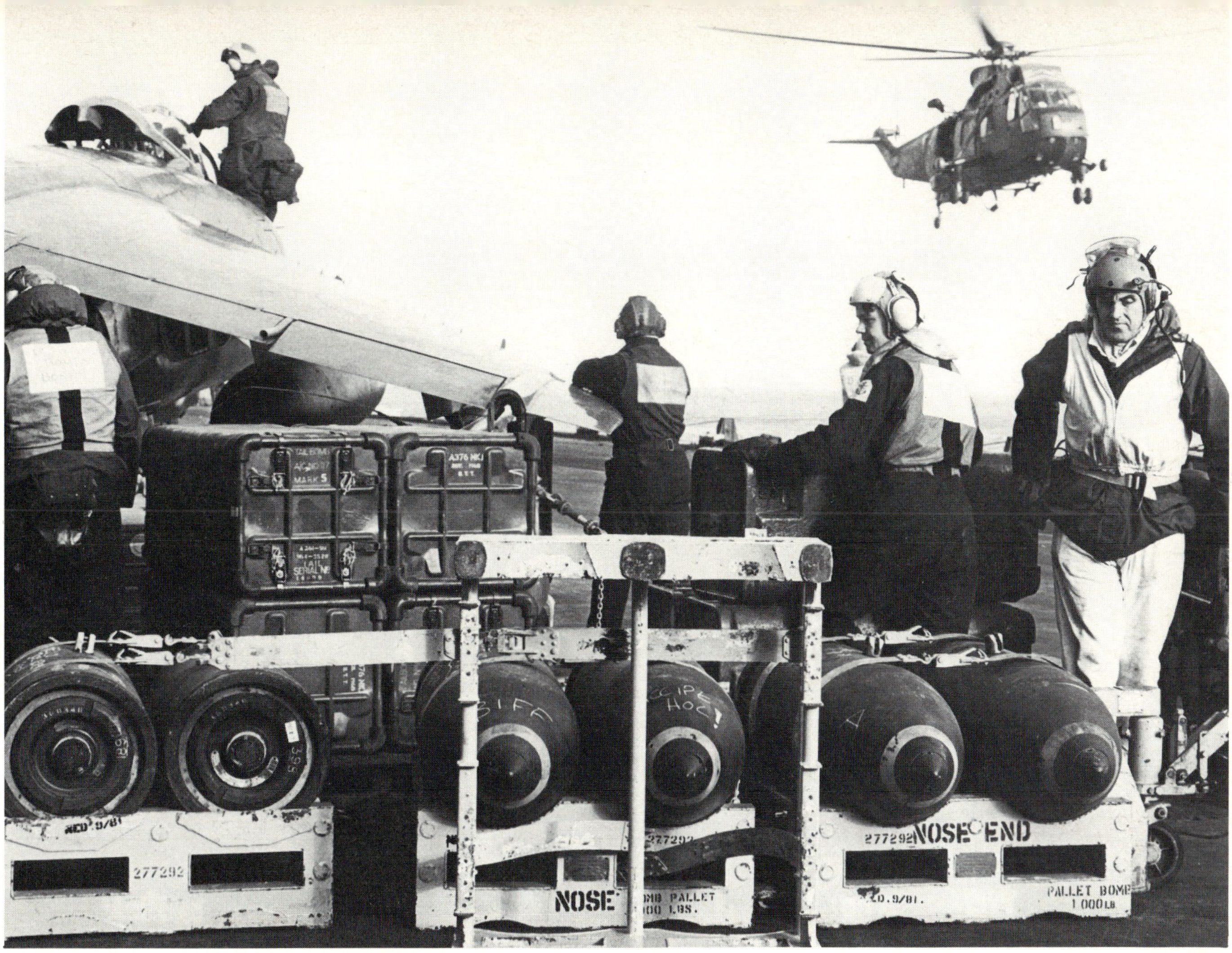
277292
NOSE END
277292
NOSE
PALLET BOMB
1 000 LB

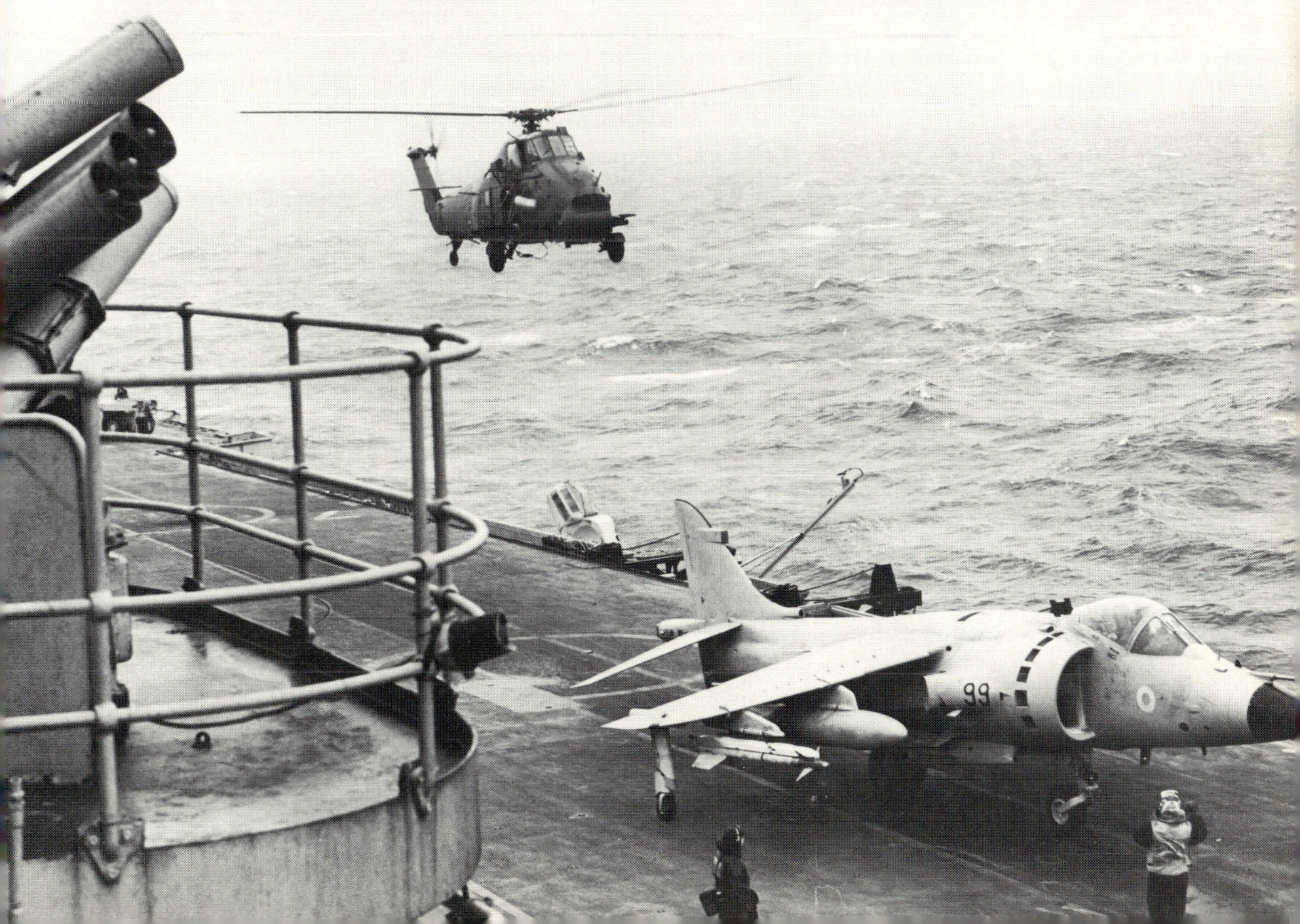
99

Above:
A rare air-to-air photograph of a Sea Harrier taken during the Falklands conflict: No 76, ZA176 of No 800 Squadron, taken with the starboard facing camera of another aircraft of the same unit.

Right:
Lt Clive Morell (*right***) and Flt Lt John Leeming of No 800 fought a successful action against a flight of three Skyhawks of 3rd Fighter and Attack Escuadrilla of the Argentine Navy on 21 May, after the latter attacked HMS *Ardent*. Morell shot down the aircraft flown by Lt-Cdr Alberto Philippi (***centre right***) with a Sidewinder ; the pilot ejected. Leeming shot down Lt Marquez, who was killed. Morell fired his second Sidewinder at the Skyhawk piloted by Lt Jose Arca (***far right***) but the missile failed to home in properly, he then loosed off a long burst with 30mm cannon but claimed no hits. In fact some of the rounds inflicted serious damage on the Skyhawk and Arca, unable to regain the mainland, flew his aircraft to Port Stanley and ejected.**
Morell, via Ethell

The explosion took off everything behind where the fin joined the fuselage, then the front end yawed violently and dropped into the water.

'That was the two rear aircraft out. Now I was rapidly overtaking the front two. Still there was no sign they knew we were after them. They were flying fairly close together, about 100yd apart. Unfortunately, when I fired the second missile my head-up display went out — I lost my magic green writing. We were down at about 50ft at this stage, still going very fast. But this time the other Sea Harrier was still behind me, he had lost sight of me. Dave had seen my missiles in flight and just aimed himself in their general direction.'

Lacking a gunsight and having fired both missiles, Dave Morgan could only put the enemy aircraft in the centre of his windscreen and let fly with cannon.

'I gave them a couple of seconds squirt with my cannon from about 1,400yd. I didn't see any hits at all, but the No 2 went into steep break to port across me. And that, as it transpired, put him right in front of Dave Smith. I followed him round, still with no gunsight, put him in the middle of my windscreen and closed from 400 to 300yd firing bursts at him; I had no real idea where my rounds were going. I didn't see any of them impact on the water. But Dave did, he saw the rounds exploding and saw the Mirage [sic] flying through the explosions down at 30-ish feet. He locked on one of his missiles, but he didn't want to fire because he didn't know where I was.

'I called "I'm out of rounds, pulling up!" I just rolled the wings horizontal and then pulled up vertically. Dave saw me go through the horizon, meanwhile the No 2 rolled his wings level as he saw me pull up and sat at about 15ft above the sea, going out to the southwest very fast. I looked over my shoulder and saw the steaming trail as Dave fired his missile, it went so low I could see the reflection of the trail on the water. Then, a few seconds later, there was a bloody great explosion over the coast at Hammond Point as the aircraft smashed into the ground.

'Dave then pulled up — by this stage we were desperately short of fuel. We joined up and returned to *Hermes*. It was 50min after sunset when we got back. I made my first night landing with 2min worth of fuel and Dave Smith had less than that.'

Like most of the Sea Harrier pilots who engaged Argentine fighter-bombers, Dave Morgan felt his opponents were reasonably competent at piloting their aircraft. But they lacked the comprehensive tactical training given to British aircrew.

'There was no indication that they understood the value of the sort of formations that we fly. When one guy was being engaged, there was no attempt by any of the other guys to come over and give him cover. It seemed that once they were engaged, it was every man for himself to get the hell out of it.

'If I was doing a low level bounce check on a new pilot who had just become operational on one of our attack squadrons in Germany and I got that sort of response, that guy would fail . . .'

Lt Steve Thomas obtained a cadetship to the Royal Navy in 1972, while he was at university reading mechanical engineering. After graduating in 1975 he went to Dartmouth naval college to train as an Engineer Officer. At the end of 1977 he was selected as a pilot for the Fleet Air Arm, for which he was sent to the Royal Air Force for flying training. He converted on to the Harrier at Wittering, and early in 1981 began the Sea Harrier course at Yeovilton. With this behind him he joined No 801 Squadron, assigned to HMS *Invincible, in May 1981. At the time of the Falklands conflict a year later he had only some 200 flying hours on the Harrier and Sea Harrier, which made him one of the least experienced of the pilots who flew these aircraft in action. This relative lack of flying experience did not inhibit him in the slightest, however. Usually he flew as wing-man to Lt-Cdr 'Sharkey' Ward, the squadron commander, and together the pair formed the most successful air fighting team during the conflict; while operating together they shot down a total of five enemy aircraft, and flying with another pilot Steve Thomas shot down one more. Although officially credited with only one confirmed 'kill' and two 'probables', from examination of Argentine records it is clear that both of his 'probables' were in fact destroyed. With two Daggers and a Mirage to his credit, he was the only British pilot to cause the destruction of three enemy fast-jets. At the time of writing he is a student on the test pilots' course at Boscombe Down.*

Steve Thomas first went into action on the afternoon on 1 May 1982, a few hours after the air fighting over the Falklands began. With another member of No 801 Squadron, Flt Lt Paul Barton, he was on patrol near West Falkland when their fighter controller on the destroyer HMS *Glamorgan* reported an incoming force of enemy aircraft. At the time Thomas made the initial radar contact on the enemy aircraft the two Sea Harriers were in standard defensive battle formation, flying in line abreast about a mile apart.

'I got the first radar pick up, so then I co-ordinated our attack. We were running in towards each other, head-on. I was doing about 400kt [460mph], Paul accelerated and pulled away to the right, to try to get around the back of them. I locked my radar on to their leader, then I began looking for the others — I couldn't believe that a pair of fighters would come in alone like that. Their formation was poor, what the Americans call "welded wing", flying very close together.'

To Thomas and Barton it seemed that the only rational reason for the Argentine behaviour was that perhaps they were co-ordinating their attack with another pair of fighters, trying to catch the Sea Harriers in a pincer movement. But try as they might, the two British pilots could find no trace of other enemy fighters launching a co-ordinated attack; and from Argentine records we know there were none. Paul Barton later commented 'This is the sort of thing one learns not to do on Day 1 at the Tactical Weapons Unit. We would never dream of flying that sort of formation, so it was mildly surprising when they did'. Still keeping a wary eye open for some possible trick, the Sea Harrier pilots closed in on the enemy aircraft from two sides as they mounted their own pincer attack.

'I got a visual at about eight miles and saw it was a Mirage. And I could also see his No 2, just to the right and behind. I was trying to lock a Sidewinder on to him but the missile would not acquire, I didn't get any growl so I couldn't fire it.

'At five miles their leader launched a missile at me, but I saw it diverge and go down to my left. At the same time something came off the second aircraft; it was tumbling, obviously a missile that had misfired. I didn't feel threatened by either missile.'

As Thomas hurtled toward the Mirages with a closing speed of over 1,000mph he eased back on the stick, dropped his wing and pulled into a turn, and saw the enemy fighters pass close underneath him.

'I began turning hard to the right, and passed about 100ft above the top of their leader. I could make out every detail of the aircraft, its camouflage pattern, and see the pilot in his cockpit. I continued my turn towards the No 2, who was about $\frac{1}{4}$mile in trail on the leader's left.'

While all this was happening Paul Barton, apparently unseen by either of the enemy pilots, was swinging round on to their tails. Steve Thomas had a ringside seat of his attack.

'As I was in the turn I passed over the top of Paul, as he was moving in to attack. I saw his guns firing. Then the rear man rolled off the bank and started a gentle climb, seemingly unaware that Paul was sitting right behind him. My impression was that these pilots were not very good, tactically. They didn't seem to know what was going on. They both seemed aware that I was there, but I don't think they knew what Paul was up to.'

But there are no prizes for the man who comes second in an air battle. Paul Barton eased his aircraft down to silhouette the enemy fighter against the cold background of the sky, locked on a Sidewinder and fired it. Still in the turn, Steve Thomas watched his comrade achieve the first aerial victory for the Sea Harrier:

'I saw the missile streak towards the No 2, it

Below:
Loading a Sea Harrier of No 801 Squadron with three 1,000lb bombs; the bomb under the starboard wing is fitted with a VT (radar) fuse in the nose to detonate it at a pre-set altitude above the ground. *Ward*

Bottom:
Flt Lt Ian Mortimer of No 801 Squadron, centre, pictured with the Sea King crew of No 820 Squadron which rescued him from the sea after his Sea Harrier was shot down by a Roland missile near Port Stanley on 1 June. Mortimer was in his dinghy off the enemy-held coast for nine hours before he was picked up. *MoD*

exploded, and the rear end of the Mirage became a big bright yellow torch. The front half of the aircraft remained more or less intact and, shedding pieces, continued on and on upwards in a ballistic trajectory.

'Meanwhile, I was continuing my turn and the enemy leader was doing quite a hard descending turn to the left, going down very fast towards the top of the solid cloud cover at 4,000ft. I'm not sure if he knew where I was. I rolled into a vertical descent behind him, locked on one of my missiles and fired it. The missile streaked after him and just

before he reached cloud I saw it pass close to his tail. Then both the aircraft and the missile vanished.'

Now running short of fuel, the two Sea Harrier pilots broke off the action and returned to *Invincible*. Afterwards Barton was credited with one confirmed kill, and Thomas with a 'probable'. The rest of the story later emerged from Argentina. The Mirage IIIs in the action belonged to Grupo 8, and the section leader was Gustavo Garcia Cuerva. After Paul Barton's missile struck his Mirage the wing man, Carlos Perona, ejected. He came down in shallow water off the north coast of West Falkland and walked ashore. He never did see either Barton's Sea Harrier or the Sidewinder, and after his rescue he reported that he thought he might have collided with one of the British fighters. This is the origin of a rather garbled account which has appeared in some journals, concerning the alleged destruction of a Sea Harrier in air-to-air combat. Garcia Cuerva's aircraft did not survive long after the destruction of his wing man. Steve Thomas's Sidewinder went off on its proximity fuse close by the Mirage and inflicted severe damage. Streaming fuel from his puncturd tanks, the pilot headed towards Port Stanley to try and land there. But as the Mirage ran in over the town from the west, trigger-happy Argentine anti-aircraft gunners opened up and blasted it out of the sky, killing the pilot. Even had the wounded fighter been able to land on the damaged and, for a Mirage, very short runway at Port Stanley, however, there is no doubt that it would never have taken off again. So from the moment the Sidewinder detonated close to the fighter it was a total loss, and this author has no hesitation in crediting the victory to Steve Thomas.

During the three weeks that followed Steve Thomas had no further encounters with the enemy. His next meeting was shortly after noon on 21 May, the day of the British landings at San Carlos Water. That morning he was airborne on a combat air patrol near the beachhead flying as wingman to Lt-Cdr 'Sharkey' Ward. With the pair was Lt-Cdr Al Craig, on his first operational sortie after coming south on *Atlantic Conveyor* with No 809 Squadron. The three fighters were at 15,000ft and nearing the end of their patrol, when their control ship HMS *Brilliant* reported she had contact with a 'slow mover' at low altitude to the south of San Carlos Water. The Sea Harriers moved into position

to investigate and Steve Thomas was first to
catch sight of the enemy aircraft, a Pucara:
'He popped out from under cloud in front of
us, going south at low level. He was over
land when I first saw him and in his light
colouring he stuck out like a sore thumb. I
told "Sharkey" I had seen him and went
down to attack. It was our policy not to
waste a Sidewinder against a Pucarra, but
even though he was going in a straight line at
low level he made a difficult shot with guns. I
went down in a descending angled-off track-
ing run from about 45 degrees to one side,
but I couldn't set his wing span into my sight
because he was flying with his wings
horizontal. I opened fire and saw my rounds
impacting on the ground all around him but I
don't know if any of them hit. Then I pulled
up and Sharkey went in. He had the right
idea, he slowed down and sat about 200yds
behind the Pucara with a low overtaking
speed and fired into him. That caused a lot of
damage and he caught fire. Al went in and
had a go. Then Sharkey went in and had
another go. By then one of the engines was
stopped and on fire. We saw the pilot eject,
then the Pucara' went on and belly landed on
its own accord.'

'Sid's Strip'. (*Top*) The Harrier forward operating base near San Carlos Settlement, constructed from AM2 aluminium matting by Royal Engineers with no heavy equipment, on unprepared ground in less than a week (*Above*) A Sea Harrier getting airborne from the strip. On 13 June the downwash from a helicopter blew away part of the aluminium matting at the landing strip, putting it out of action temporarily. At the time Lt–Cdr Neil Thomas and Lt Simon Hargreaves of No 800 Squadron were on combat air patrol in the area, planning to land on the strip to refuel. Neither aircraft had sufficient fuel to return to *Hermes*, but they were able to make emergency landings on the helicopter decks of the assault ships *Fearless* and *Invincible* at anchor in San Carlos Water. Had the pilots been flying conventional fixed-wing aircraft in such circumstances, they would have had to eject and the aircraft would have been lost. (*Right*) Simon Hargreaves landing on *Intrepid*. *MoD*

After the action the three Sea Harriers, by now short of fuel, climbed back to high altitude and returned to *Invincible*. The Pucara pilot, Maj Juan Tomba of Grupo 3, parachuted to the ground without injury and walked back to Goose Green.

Steve Thomas and 'Sharkey' Ward flew a second mission that day, without incident. Then at 14.20, local Falklands time, the pair took off again. For Steve Thomas it was to be the most eventful mission of the conflict. As they neared the landing area 'Sharkey' Ward called *Brilliant* for instructions and Steve Thomas recalled:

'Her controller was speaking to us, he said there was a raid coming in. Then we heard several "clonks" on the radio. There was a pause, then the controller said, "We've just been hit! ... Hang on a minute ... The guy next to me has been hit in the stomach and I've been hit on the arm". (Despite his injury, this controller remained at his post until darkness fell.)

'We were not allowed into the San Carlos area without special clearance, and then only when there were no enemy aircraft present, because the area was designated a Missile Engagement Zone where the ships could engage without having to identify first. So we

mounted a patrol near Pebble Island hoping to catch the enemy aircraft as they came away from their target.

'Sharkey decided we would go down to low level and search over the north-eastern end of West Falkland, just to the north of Mount Maria. We were flying at between 500 and 1,000ft above ground level, going quite slowly at about 300kt [345mph]. We reached the southern end of the patrol line and started a starboard turn back on to north. I looked down under my aircraft and there were two Daggers, big yellow strips on their wings, going underneath me. They were in a low-level attack formation, about 500yd apart in echelon, going very fast.

'I barrelled in behind them, locked up a missile on the rear guy and fired. The Sidewinder hit the aircraft and took it apart. I didn't see it go in, I was busy trying to get the other one. He went into a climbing turn to starboard to try to get away. I locked up a Sidewinder and fired it. The missile followed him round the corner and went close over his port wing root. There was a bright orange flash close to the aircraft but it didn't blow up or anything.

'Then Sharkey called up and said he had contact with another hostile and was firing a missile. I looked back in his direction, saw the missile in flight and in front of it was another Dagger. It was going at a slight oblique angle past us, about a mile away. The missile scored a direct hit on it, and it broke up into bits.

'Almost immediately afterwards *Brilliant* called up and said there were some A4s passing through Falkland Sound. We got back into formation, with just one missile between us, and headed east. As we reached Port Howard we went on either side of the settlement, to avoid the Argentine troop positions there. But I must have flown over one of the outlying machine-gun posts because suddenly I saw small orange flashes coming past me. A split second later there was the sound of a "thump" on the radio and at the same time one of my fuel pumps failed. Both of my radios were out.'

Now separated from his leader and with no means of regaining contact, Steve Thomas began climbing out to the east to make his way back to the carrier. As he moved clear of the enemy, however a new danger emerged: that he might be engaged by 'friendly' missiles from the ships as he neared the Task Force.

'I returned at high altitude. I had my IFF on of course, but I didn't know whether it was still working. I did not want to set my IFF to "emergency", because apart from the radios my aircraft was OK and it might have made the carriers over-react. We had a pre-briefed pattern to fly in case of a radio failure. I went through this procedure, using the briefed IFF settings. The whole time I kept a beady eye on the radar warning receiver screen to make sure no "friendly" radar was trying to lock on to me! But fortunately there were no problems.

'When I reached the carrier I went into the hover, and there was the Flight Deck Officer in his yellow jacket pointing at the spot on which I was to land.

'After I landed I found the aircraft had been hit in the avionics compartment at the rear by three .5in armour piercing rounds. Two had gone clean through the fuselage and come out the top, one had lodged in the TACAN control box. From the direction in which the bullets hit, the enemy machine gun must have been almost exactly underneath me.'

When they landed, each of the pilots confirmed the destruction of the other's Dagger. But because neither had seen Steve Thomas's second target crash, this could be claimed only as 'possibly destroyed' For the second time in the conflict the young pilot had claimed an enemy aircraft in this way; and, again, the author is able to confirm from Argentine records that the aircraft he engaged was destroyed. In the action Grupo 6 lost three Daggers. In view of the low altitude and high speed of the engagement, it is indeed remarkable that the pilots of all three Argentine fighter-bombers — Maj Piuma, Capt Donadile and Lt Senn — were all able to eject safely.

Again there was a period, this time of 10 days, in which Steve Thomas had no further contact with enemy aircraft. Then, on the morning of 1 June, he was again on patrol with 'Sharkey' Ward in the area of San Carlos Water.

'HMS *Minerva*, the San Carlos control ship that day, had picked up a couple of glimpses on radar of a contact about 20 miles north of Pebble Island, then lost it. Sharkey and I were sent to investigate. We went after the contact, assuming it had gone back to low level because the ship could no longer see it. Sharkey picked up the aircraft on radar, by then it was heading west. We thought it

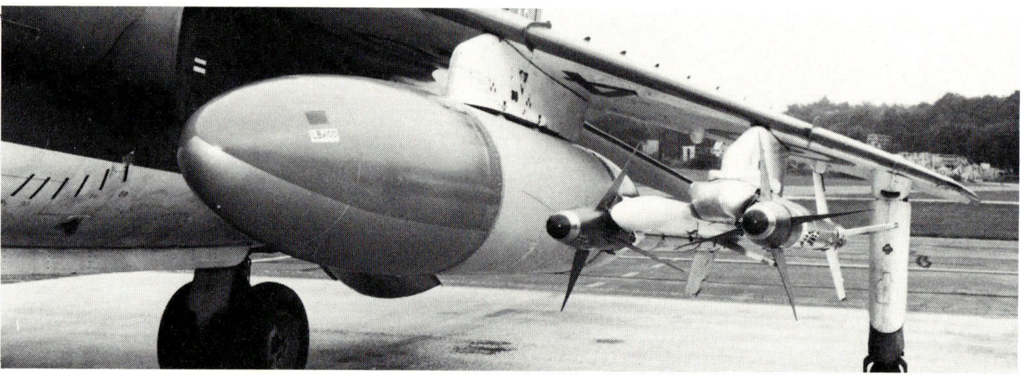

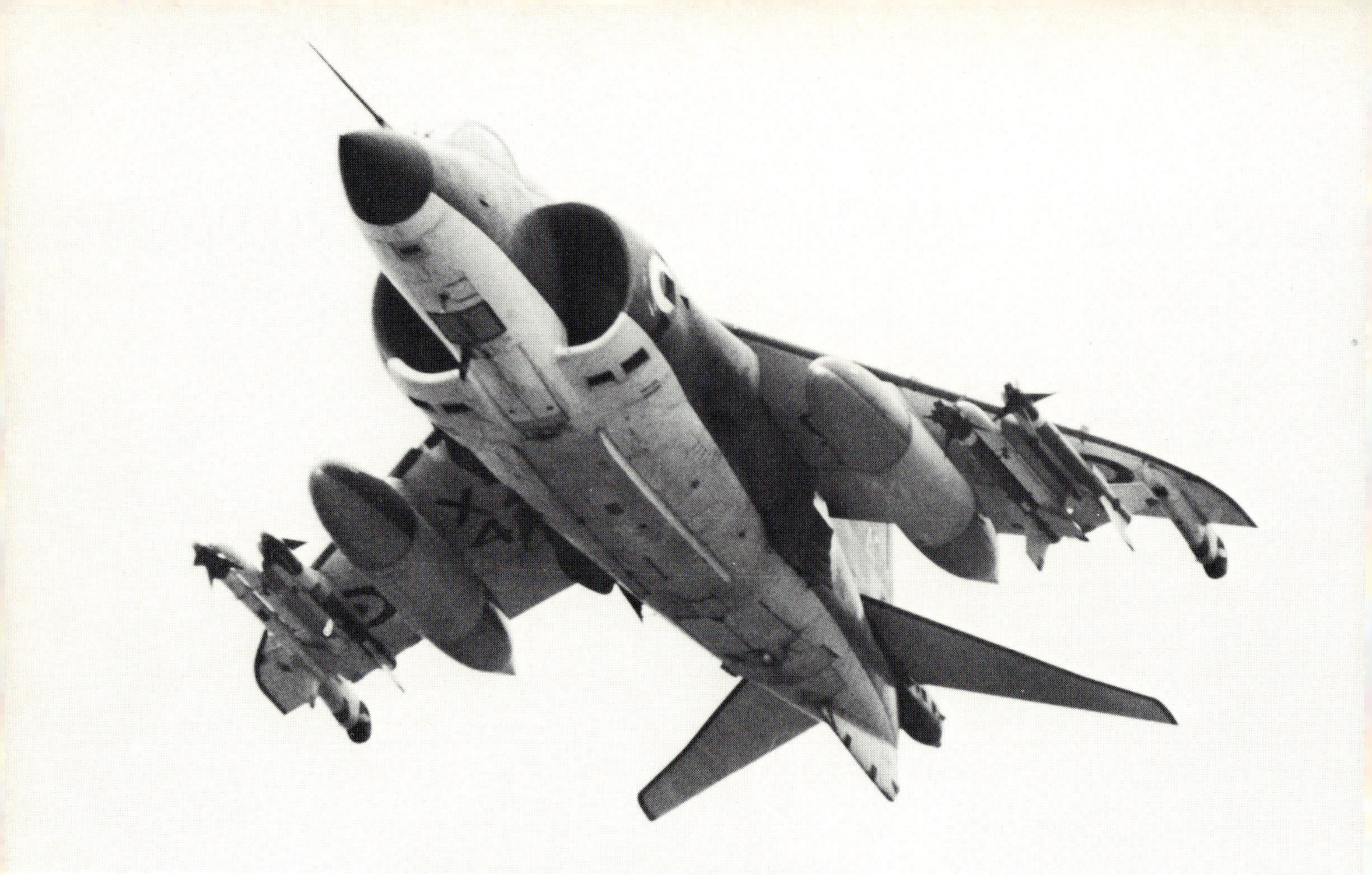

This page:
Sea Harrier modifications completed just too late for action in the South Atlantic: with twin-racks for Sidewinder, to enable the aircraft to carry four of these missiles; and larger, 190gal, drop tanks to increase the aircraft's endurance during combat missions.

might be a C-130 because of its low speed. Sharkey went down through the cloud layer to engage, I stayed above it at 3,000ft in case the aircraft had top cover. Then Sharkey called that he had a Hercules in sight at a range of about six miles, and I went down to join him. I emerged from cloud to see a missile leaving his aircraft, and out in front I could make out the Hercules at about 200ft going flat out. There was no sign that the Hercules crew had seen Sharkey, we had gone radar silent so as not to warn them.'

Being short of fuel Ward had fired his missile at extreme range, just too far from the target as it turned out.

'The missile was about to hit the aircraft when suddenly it dropped away and fell into the water. By then Sharkey was much closer and he fired a second, which hit between the engines on the starboard wing, which immediately burst into flames. Still the aircraft kept going so Sharkey went in closer still and emptied his guns into it. The Hercules went into a descending turn out of control to starboard, the wing struck the sea and it cartwheeled and broke up.'

All six members of the crew of the Hercules, an aircraft of Grupp 1 which was on its way back from Port Stanley, were killed.

'All of this happened 20-30 miles north of Pebble Island, and by the end of it we were very short of fuel. As we broke away we had the option of landing on the decks of *Fearless* and *Intrepid* in San Carlos Water. We calculated our fuel remaining and the consumption very carefully, we had a tail wind, the weather was very good and we worked out that we could get back to our carrier. We flew back at 35,000ft, then began our descent to the ship. With the throttle shut you can let the speed build up, you do not need to open the throttle again until you turn finals. We did a pairs break abeam the ship, a quick circuit and then went in to land. When I touched down I had 300-350lb of fuel left. The deck of a landing ship was a fall-back option, which we did not need to take up on this occasion.'

A week later, at dusk on 8 June, Steve Thomas and Sharkey Ward nearly went into action yet again. As Dave Morgan and Dave Smith from No 800 Squadron were engaging the Skyhawks of Grupo 5 off Choiseul Sound, shooting down three of them, Thomas and Ward were moving up from the south to cut off the survivor.
'We were about 10 miles to the south, going in to help. We saw the missiles' trails as they went after the aircraft and hit them. Then the guard ship HMS *Cardiff* at San Carlos called up and said there were other targets coming in from the west. So we had to break away and move west to meet them. We saw them at about 30 miles, they were contrailing and they came straight for us. We gulped a bit at the thought of going up after those guys, we were at 20,000ft and they were up at 35,000. But as we got to within 10 miles they turned away; we could see their Mirage shape quite clearly.'

Although they had no way of knowing it at the time, the two pilots had witnessed one of the rare appearances of air-to-air missile armed Mirage IIIs of Grupo 8 over the Falklands after the action on 1 May. But, having learned their lesson during the earlier action, the unit kept well out of the reach of the Sea Harriers.

When the conflict ended on 14 June, despite press reports to the contrary, *none* of the Sea Harrier pilots had ever had the opportunity or the need to make use of their aircraft's unique VIFF (thrust Vectored In Forward Flight) capability in combat. Of this facility Steve Thomas comments:
'VIFFing is something you would use against a fast aeroplane, if he is menacing you from behind. You would use it to slow down very rapidly, usually combined with some sort of barrel roll, so that he will overtake and leave you sitting behind him. But we were never menaced in this particular manner by the enemy pilots. It would have been pointless to use VIFF, because one of its major effects is that it slows you down and uses up all the aircraft's energy. In air-to-air combat you don't want to be low on energy, because that could allow the other guy to "eat you up". So we never had cause to use VIFF during the conflict.'

Steve Thomas is the first to admit that his high score is largely a result of his happening to be in the right place at the right time. Other pilots were less fortunate.
'There were two very experienced and capable guys on our squadron, Flt Lt Ian Mortimer and Lt Charlie Cantan, who seemed often to arrive on station just as the action was finishing or had finished, or would have to return short of fuel just as something was about to happen. They never had a chance to go into action, they were never on station when the Argentine fighter-bombers came through.'

On the other hand, luck in air combat is usually of little avail unless pilots have the skill, determination and means to exploit it. There can be no doubt that during the conflict Steve Thomas made the very most of his opportunities. And it says a lot for the Sea Harrier/AIM-9L combination that such a relatively junior pilot was able to achieve the results he did.
Having fought in the Sea Harrier, what are Steve Thomas's feelings about the aircraft?
'The Sea Harrier is a superb aircraft, well designed for the way it was conceived — a cheap naval fighter derivative of the Royal Air Force's Harrier GR3. The conflict has certainly demonstrated the operational flexibility of the Sea Harrier. The aircraft does not need any special radar or other equipment on the ship for it to land in bad weather or at night; approaches are made using the ship's navigation radar. Also we did not need a catapult, arrester gear, lots of wind etc.
'I think our high serviceability and the way we were able to get a very large proportion of our aircraft airborne was a reflection on the excellence of our maintainers. They were helped by the fact that it was a war situation and the spares were forthcoming — which, normally, sometimes they are not. It meant that even with a small force, we managed to keep a lot of aircraft airborne day and night.'

Flt Lt Tony Harper was a member of the No 1 Squadron 'first team', the group of pilots which went south initially and flew the Harrier GR3 on operations from HMS Hermes. *In the spring of 1982 he was on his third flying tour, having completed one on Harriers in Germany and another instructing on Hunters at the Tactical Weapons Unit as Lossiemouth. When he left for the South Atlantic he had 865 hours flying time on Harriers, which was about average for the pilots on the 'first team'. At the time of writing he is an instructor at No 233 Operational Conversion Unit at Wittering, teaching new pilots to fly the Harrier. In this account he tells of the events which preceded the squadron's move to the South Atlantic, his operations over the Falklands and the lessons he learned from them.*

'About a week after the Argentine invasion of the Falklands it began to dawn on us that No 1 Squadron was likely to become involved. There were lots of comings and goings, and we began to get the idea that perhaps we were going somewhere. Sqn Ldr Bob Iveson went off to look at *Atlantic Conveyor* to see if she was suitable to take Harriers. At first we thought we were going to be put on a ship in this country and taken all the way to the South Altantic, where we would then lift across to one of the carriers.'

Gradually the No 1 Squadron pilots learned what was in store for them: they were to fly to Ascension Island, put their aircraft on the deck of the container ship *Atlantic Conveyor* which would carry them to the South Atlantic, lift across to HMS *Hermes* and fly from her deck.

'On 15 April we flew to Yeovilton to practice taking off from the ski-jump. It was very impressive. The jump at Yeovilton was set at seven degrees, the same as those on *Illustrious* and *Invincible* whereas the one we were to use on *Hermes* is set at 12 degrees. But it gave a fair impression of what the ski-jump take off would be like. It was absolutely no problem, the psychological reassurance of having done it was excellent.'

Throughout the planning for Operation 'Corporate', the combined operation to retake the Falkland Islands, the biggest single equipment limitation on the British side was the shortage of Sea Harriers: only 28 were available to go south, and each one lost would seriously deplete the air cover for the ships of the Task Force. In the limited time available no more Sea Harriers could be manufactured, the only other possibility was to use Royal Air Force Harrier GR3s in the interceptor role. Thus, in addition to having to learn to operate from the deck of an aircraft carrier, the No 1 Squadron pilots had also to prepare themselves for the unfamiliar role of flying as interceptor fighters: they

were to seek battle with enemy aircraft (which was quite different from the attack pilots' accustomed role of avoiding air-to-air combat whenever possible and fighting only when they had to).

'At this time we were expecting to go down as fighters, the aircraft were being modified to carry Sidewinder missiles. We were doing our homework on Sidewinder performance, firing parameters and that sort of thing. We had a programme of lectures and briefings. And we each went off to Valley and each fired a missile at a drone over Cardigan Bay.

Also we did some dissimilar air combat training with Phantoms and Lightnings. If you are going to war you cannot get enough dissimilar air combat training.'

Still as part of the preparations for Operation 'Corporate', on 20 and 23 April Tony Harper conducted the trial firings of the naval 2in rocket from the Harrier. This was the first time the RAF aircraft had carried this weapon. The normal load was two pods of rockets, one under either wing; each of the naval pods carried 36 2in rockets, whereas the RAF pods housed 19 of the 68mm missiles.

'There were no problems, except that the aeroplane feels heavier because the 2in rocket pods are heavier than the SNEB pods. After the rockets have been fired you can feel the basic weight of the empty pod is higher than the empty weight of the SNEB pod.'

On 29 April Tony Harper flew a training mission over Wales flying the Harrier at altitudes down to 100ft. If the Squadron was to go to war, the ability to fly low would be vital to the survival of its pilots.

'If somebody is pointing a radar, a missile or a gun at you, you need to put something physical between you and him. In nine cases out of ten, the best thing is going to be a hill. So you look for the blind spot on the other side of the hill from the weapon or the radar; if the hill is 1,000ft high, you need to fly only

900ft above the ground on the other side of that hill. But if the hill is only 50ft high, you have to be at 30ft on the other side of the hill. In normal training we are allowed down to 250ft. Exceptionally we are allowed to train down to 100ft, but no lower because of the risk to the aircraft. Anti-aircraft weapons, missiles and guns, are sited on hills to give good coverage. But the look-down performance of most weapons is very limited. So the lower you can fly, the better your chances of survival.

'The problem of flying at 600kts [690mph] at 100ft is that it feels as if you are flying through a "tunnel". There is a segment of about 15 degrees either side of the nose of the aircraft where you can see clearly; on either side of the ground is just a blur. Because you are looking through that "tunnel", and you are so close to the ground, you dare not look anywhere else but where you are going. There is no time to look at a map. You certainly cannot look over your shoulder for possible enemy aircraft which may drop in behind you, or cover the rear of your wing man.

'The first time I flew that low at high speed, it really did put the wind up me. For the first 10 hours' flying at low altitude, you are able to do nothing but look straight in front of you and fly. However, with practice, you get more comfortable at it. And when you are used to it, you can devote more attention to doing the other things that need to be done.

'If you are flying a sortie to 100ft, the briefing is "not below 100ft", not to fly *at*

100ft. Basically, you fly as low as you need to fly. So you plan the route taking into account the terrain over which you are flying, and tune in your mind to those parts of it where you will need to go that low. Maybe the approach for the first 30 miles of the route to the target is over friendly territory and you are shielded from the enemy by a line of hills. Then you can fly at 500ft. But where you might be exposed to enemy radars or defences, you have to come down.'

By the end of April the No 1 Squadron pilots knew they were going south, the only question was 'When?' On 2 May the initial wave of six aircraft left Wittering for St Mawgan in Cornwall, from where they were to fly to Ascension Island.

'When we got to St Mawgan there was a crosswind which was outside limits for Harriers making conventional-type landings. We were carrying the big ferry tanks on the inboard pylons and small tanks on the outer pylons; and with those on the Harrier cannot land vertically because the tanks are too heavy and cause all sorts of problems during the deceleration into the hover.'

The conventional answer would have been to go somewhere else where the crosswinds were lower, or jettison the ferry tanks; but both of these courses of action would have jeopardised the operation to ferry the aircraft to Ascension Island, planned for the following day. In the event the pilots solved the problem by ignoring it.

'The "release to service" limits of the Harrier were suddenly increased, we gritted out teeth and landed anyway! We did "slow landings", coming over the hedge at 160kts [185mph] and using reverse thrust to slow the aircraft after touchdown.'

On the following morning, 3 May, Wg Cdr Peter Squire led Tony Harper and Flt Lt Mark Hare off from St Mawgan for the long flight to Ascension.

'We joined up with a couple of Victor tankers off the coast of Cornwall and off we went. After giving up the rest of its spare fuel to the other Victor over the Bay of Biscay, one of the tankers turned back for home. The other one went with us as far as the bump on the west coast of Africa. At that point there was a problem: the tanker crew found they did not have enough fuel to get all the Harriers to Ascension. So the Boss decided that he would go to Banjul [in The Gambia] with the tanker and refuel there.

'Mark Hare and I were left to find our own way to Ascension, from a point 1,200 miles north of the island. There were no real problems, it was just boring: nothing else to do but steer the perishing aeroplane for 9 hr 15 min. When we arrived, the first three beers didn't touch the sides!'

Although there was little recognition of it at the time, the pilots had just broken the world record for a non-stop flight in a V/STOL aircraft; the previous longest had been 6hr 15min, from Wittering to Goose Bay in Labrador. Peter Squire arrived on Ascension later in the evening, just after achieving the unenviable distinction of spending a record 13 hours either in the cockpit of a Harrier or

Above:
Scene on *Atlantic Conveyor*, after the aircraft had been loaded. As well as the six Harriers of No 1 Squadron there were eight Sea Harriers of No 809 Squadron. Also visible on deck were a Chinook and five Wessex helicopters, the former and three of the latter in protective bags.

from Ascension and landed on *Atlantic Conveyor* lying at anchor just off the coast. That evening the container ship set sail for the south Atlantic, for what was to be her final voyage. The Harriers of No 1 Squadron, together with eight Sea Harriers of 809 Squadron, seven Wessex, a Lynx and four Chinook helicopters, travelled south on the deck of the container ship. On 18 May *Atlantic Conveyor* made a rendezvous with the British naval task force and began to transfer her Harriers and Sea Harriers to the aircraft carriers. Two of the Harriers were unservicable, however, including Tony Harper's which had a starter failure. The groundcrew set about curing the faults and he and Flt Lt John Rochfort flew their aircraft over to HMS *Hermes* on the 19th and 20th respectively.

On arrival on *Hermes* the Royal Air Force Harriers were still configured as interceptors, and during their initial flights to familiarise pilots with deck operations the aircraft carried AIM-9G Sidewinder missiles. With the landings on the Falklands due to begin on the night of 20 May, however, and the Sea Harrier losses somewhat lower than had been feared, the Royal Air Force GR3s were reconfigured back to the ground attack role. The GR3s flew their first mission on the afternoon of the 20th, when Wg Cdr Squire led his two flight commanders, Sqn Ldrs Jerry Pook and Bob Iveson, in a three-aircraft attack on an Argentine fuel dump at Fox Bay on West Falkland. Tony Harper did not take part in a mission over the Falklands until the following day.

'My first operation was on the 21st, when I went to the airfield at Dunnose Head on an armed reconnaissance with Sqn Ldr Pook. The aircraft carried cluster bombs, but we didn't find anything to attack.

'After the initial missions, in which first Mark Hare came back with hits and then Jeff Glover failed to return, we decided we would have to fly lower and faster in future. We developed our tactics to fit the situation at the time. We would arrive at high level to make the most of our fuel, then let-down going away from the target to spoof the Argentine radar operators into thinking we were going somewhere else. Then we relied on the ultra-low flying to bring us back towards the target without being seen by the radars. Whenever we were within about 30 miles of Port Stanley, if we were attacking targets in that area, we would be down at about 100ft.

close beside one as his aircraft was refuelled at Banjul.

'When we got to Ascension everybody was working flat-out. The second part of the Task Force, with the amphibious forces, was just arriving. *Atlantic Conveyor* was due to arrive that night, *Canberra* was due to arrive shortly. Everybody was busy rushing around, helicopters were moving stores, loading ships. Aeroplanes were coming in full of people, and going off all through the day and night. The Vulcans were setting up their raids on Port Stanley. We had a short wait for the rest of the Squadron, we were given some accommodation and told "Go away, we'll call when we want you!" '

On 4 May the second wave of three Harriers arrived on Ascension, and on the 5th three more. On 6 May six of the Harriers took off

Above:
Close-up of the combat-ready Sea Harrier on *Atlantic Conveyor*, during an engine run. Had it been needed for an interception the aircraft would have taken off vertically but could carry little fuel — note the lack of external tanks. To extend its range, the aircraft carried a refuelling probe and would have had to take fuel from a Victor tanker kept orbiting near the ship during the initial part of her voyage south.

Left:
Pilots of the No 1 Squadron 'First Team' pictured on *Atlantic Conveyor* on their way to the south Atlantic: from left to right, standing, Sqn Ldr Peter Harris, Flt Lt Jeff Glover, Flt Lt Mark Hare, Flt Lt John Rochfort, Sqn Ldr Jerry Pook, Wg Cdr Peter Squire and Sqn Ldr Bob Iveson; sitting, Flt Lt Tony Harper. *Harper*

91

'Initially we thought there was going to be a high threat of attack from enemy fighters. We very quickly discovered that there was no threat from the air, so at low altitude we stopped flying what we called a mutually supporting formation — in line abreast, with each pilot searching behind the other for enemy fighters. We ended up flying in search formations, almost in line astern, so that the leader could identify the target in time to tell the No 2 where it was, so that the latter could get his weapons on to it in case the leader's missed.

'We never got blasé about the threat from enemy fighters however. Every morning we were told: their guys are bound to twig some time, and come and have a fight. So we briefed very carefully what we were going to do if we met enemy fighters at high altitude. Basically, we were going to stand our aircraft on their noses, and go straight down to about 500ft and fight them on our terms down there. If you roll the Harrier on its back and pull back on the nozzles, you will put it into the vertical and go down very quickly indeed. But in the event their fighters never came near us.'

This page:
18 May 1982: *Atlantic Conveyor* delivers her Sea Harriers and Harriers to the Task Force (*Above*) Sea Harrier landing on *Hermes*; although fitted with drop tanks, the aircraft carries no missiles or launchers. On leaving the container ship No 809 Squadron ceased to exist and its aircraft and pilots were split between Nos 800 and 801 Squadrons. (*Below*) Wg Cdr Peter Squire climbing out of GR3 XZ872, after landing the first of these aircraft on *Hermes*.

Far right:
Wg Cdr Peter Squire taking off from *Hermes* on the afternoon of 20 May, to lead Sqn Ldrs Jerry Pook and Bob Iveson on the initial strike by Harrier GR3s against an Argentine fuel dump at Fox Bay on West Falkland. (*Below*) The fuel dump at Fox Bay photographed before the attack from a Sea Harrier, showing (right) the lines of 45gal drums awaiting burial. The GR3s each attacked the dump with two BL755 cluster bombs, and started large fires. *MoD*

Tony Harper flew on an armed reconnaissance with Wg Cdr Squire to Weddell Island on the 22nd, and took part in a four-aircraft attack on the airfield at Dunnose Head on the 23rd. So far he had not come under fire from the enemy, but on the next day he received his baptism during an attack on Port Stanley airfield. For this mission two Sea Harriers of No 800 Squadron were to approach the target from the northeast and toss radar airburst fused bombs to explode over the anti-aircraft gun positions and distract the defenders; and immediately afterwards two pairs of Harriers of No 1 Squadron were to run in from the northwest and west to attack the runway with parachute retarded 1,000lb bombs.

'The 24th: my first big one, take off 1855Z [1555 local time] against Port Stanley. I was Bob Iveson's No 2. As we came in we saw mushrooms of smoke in the sky, from the Sea Harriers' VT [radar airburst] fused bombs. We did not go through the target particularly fast on that raid because we were trying to bomb as accurately as possible; we flew about 480-500kt [550-575mph] , almost "tunnel vision" speed. We ran in to attack

from the northwest, going across the runway towards the control tower. I followed Bob in, he was offset to one side, about half a mile in front and 45 degrees out of my left. He was to straddle the runway about half way up, I was briefed to try and straddle the runway about a quarter of the way up. In fact I got my nearest bomb on the western edge, just off the end. I just missed the runway and caused no real damage.

'During my attack run I saw somebody standing on the control tower "at the end of the tunnel" pointing something at me with flashes coming out of it. But I was not seriously fired at, it was exciting without being dangerous.

'Afterwards we were angry that we had not inflicted any serious damage on the runway and might have to go and do the attack again. But then we wondered about the futility of attacking a runway with the sort of weapons we had. If you are going to attack a runway you need a weapon that will impact at a steep angle and not go off until it has gone through the surface; and parachute retarded 1,000 pounders don't do that, they go off as soon as they hit.'

Being fired at by the enemy during an attack on a target was bad enough, but at least a pilot could see what was going on and do something to avoid the enemy fire. Back on *Hermes*, when she came under attack, the aircrew felt completely helpless and vulnerable. Tony Harper was on the carrier on the afternoon of 25 May when the ship had her closest brush with an Exocet missile.

'I was in the aircrew room under the back end of the island when the Exocet attack was launched against the ships. The hooter sounded and we had to stay where we were. The sailors shut all the doors and we put on our anti-flash kit. Then I just sat in a chair and waited. I felt so helpless, there was nothing for me to do. We could hear the chaff rockets being fired from the ship, a series of very loud bangs overhead. There was so much happening, but there was no air of panic. We waited and waited, and about 10min later somebody came down from the deck and said that one of our ships had been hit; and later still the word came down that it was *Atlantic Conveyor*. Afterwards I was saddened to hear of the death of her master, Captain North. He was a wonderful man,

very friendly and every inch a sailor. He was short and rotund with a white beard: people called him "Captain Birdseye" after the happy sailor in the Birdseye advert, and that summed him up.'

There was no time to brood on the loss, however, No 1 Squadron had a war to fight. On the next day, the 26th, Tony Harper was No 2 to Sqn Ldr Bob Iveson during an attack with cluster bombs on Argentine troop positions at Port Howard. And on the 27th he took part in the low altitude toss-bombing attack on Port Stanley airfield; during a mission later that day, Bob Iveson failed to return from an attack on troop positions near Goose Green.

On 28 May Tony Harper was one of the participants in the three-aircraft attack on Argentine artillery positions at Goose Green, immediately in front of the advancing British paratroopers.

'I was No 2 to Sqn Ldr Peter Harris. We had been briefed to go to Goose Green, where we knew the Paras were having a push and there was a fight on. Because that was where Nick Taylor [the pilot of the Sea Harrier lost on

Left:
Proof of claim. Burned out remains of an Argentine Army Chinook destroyed by Flt Lt Mark Hare on Mount Kent early on the morning of 21 May. *Hare*

Below:
The nearest thing to a carrier landing accident by a No 1 Squadron Harrier happened on 21 May during the unit's operations from *Hermes*: photo (*left*) taken seconds after Flt Lt John Rochford bounced heavily and ended up with his port outrigger just off the flight deck. The pilot had been making his *second ever* carrier landing, returning to the ship with bombs after an uneventful armed reconnaissance mission over East Falkland. Naval deck crewmen immediately clambered on the wing of the aircraft (*right*) to prevent it falling over. The aircraft was towed back on deck with damage only to the port cluster bomb which had to be 'tested for buoyancy' (Naval parlance for 'dropped into the sea'). Despite their hasty training, the RAF pilots adapted quickly to deck operations and there were no further incidents. *MoD*

4 May] and Bob Iveson had been shot down, we expected a lot of opposition when we went in. So we were not looking forward to it. But we planned a good attack route, well shielded by the terrain.'

As well as keeping clear of the enemy defences during their run in to the target, the pilots had other points to consider:
'You have to take into account where the sun will be — you don't want it in your eyes during an attack. Then there is the wind — if you are attacking with cluster bombs you want the wind on your nose or on your tail; the errors are far greater if there is a crosswind. The attack direction has to take into account the layout of the target, to get the maximum coverage of the target with the types of weapon you are using. Also you want to release the bombs as you are moving away from your own troops to minimise the chances of your bombs hitting them — that is most important.'

Harris led the force towards the islands at 25,000ft in standard defensive battle formation with Jerry Pook behind and to the left and Tony Harper behind and to the right. The pilots maintained station about a mile apart, scanning the sky for possible enemy fighters. After making radio contact with the forward air controller at Goose Green, the small force descended to low altitude over Falkland Sound. The Harriers accelerated to attack speed and swept in towards their target from the north-north-west.

'At high altitude on the way in we made radio contact with the forward air controller and had time to look at our target maps. So we had everything squared away as we ran in at low altitude across the sea at about 50ft. In the distance we could see the thin columns of smoke rising above the battlefield, it looked like the aftermath of a battle. It all looked so very peaceful, the water was nice and smooth. Everything seemed more relaxed than during previous attacks; we had planned the route carefully, it was all on the rails and we were going for the target. We left the initial point at Terra Motas Point knowing exactly what we were going to do.

'There was hardly any wind, I remember seeing the smoke from the burning gorse on the battlefield rising almost vertically. Conditions were absolutely ideal. The target was easy to find: the buildings led us to it. We went to the left of them, we were particularly conscious that the Falkland Islanders were in the buildings and we did not want to hit them. About a mile before we passed the houses we started the pull up to release our cluster bombs. Still everything was going as planned, nobody seemed to be firing at us.

'Peter Harris was to my right and ahead, he was going to get there first and hopefully would give me some sort of correction. He dropped his weapons, I saw the cluster bomblets going off. Then he called up and said "Drop your's to the right". After we went through Jerry Pook came in from the north and attacked with his pods of 2in rockets at approximately a right angle to our heading. This gave a dense coverage of bomblets and rockets on the target.'

From other sources, we know that the attack on the Argentine artillery positions at Goose Green was completely successful. Watching from a hill to the north of the target Maj Chris Keeble, commanding 2nd Battalion of the Parachute Regiment after the death of Col 'H' Jones earlier in the day, saw the aircraft sweep in low over the ground and launch their bombs and rockets at the target. 'The attack gave a great boost to the morale of our troops. I think some of them thought the Harriers had come in a bit too close for comfort, but that is war,' he later commented. 'After that there was a marked slackening in the fighting, which had gone on very fiercely the whole day. Afterwards I sat down and thought, "Where have we got to now? What is the enemy thinking?" I tried to assess the situation from his point of view.

Now he was encircled and we had demonstrated that we could bring in the Harriers and attack his positions surgically. It was then I began to get the notion that their will had broken and maybe we could go for a surrender.' Keeble's analysis proved right: on the following morning the Argentine troops surrendered. The paratroops were amazed to discover that the force they had defeated outnumbered them by more than two to one.

The close air support mission at Goose Green had been a textbook example of this type of operation: a hard-hitting surprise attack against a target of great importance to the enemy, launched at a crucial time in the land battle, with results that could clearly be seen by the ground troops — to strengthen the resolve of those on one side and demoralise those on the other.

Tony Harper flew further missions on 30 and 31 May, then followed four days of poor weather at the beginning of June which bought a halt to the attack operations. On 5 June the squadron resumed its offensive support missions, and some of the aircraft began flying from the forward operating base near San Carlos Settlement constructed by army engineers. For Tony Harper the next memorable mission took place on 12 June, when he and Flt Lt Nick Gilchrist were sent to the Port Stanley area on an armed reconnaissance.

'By this time Wg Cdr Fred Trowern [the senior RAF liaison officer on the Falklands] was sitting on top of Mount Kent. We had very good communications, he told us he wanted an armed reconnaissance of the road from Bluff Cove to Stanley. So we did just that. We had a start point beyond which, in theory, there were none of our troops.

'Just south of Sapper Hill we found a force of Argentine troops in the open, moving

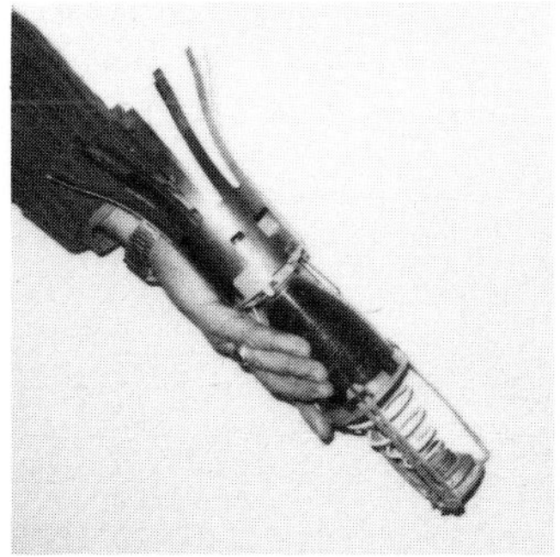

Above:
Harrier GR3s with Sea Harriers lined up on the deck of *Hermes*. The aircraft nearest the camera has two BL755 cluster bombs on the outer wing pylons and a reconnaissance pod under the fuselage. (*Below*) A BL755 cluster bomblet; 147 of these were carried, folded, in the bomb container and released after the weapon left the aircraft.
MoD, Author's collection

along the road towards Port Stanley. As I ran in to attack them with cluster bombs, I saw blokes hurling themselves flat and diving into ditches. Nick following me in, and he said my bombs went in the right area and it looked a pretty good attack. He put down his bombs in the same place. Afterwards I discovered I had collected three hits from small arms fire during the attack, though none was serious. One went through the leading edge of the wing, one through the left of the fuselage and one through the rear fuselage.'

That mission proved to be Tony Harper's final one, and two days later the Argentine forces on the Falklands surrendered. Looking back on the conflict, what does he feel are the main lessons?
'I think the main lesson of the conflict is that the training we do in the Royal Air Force is as realistic as we can make it in peacetime. The work-up immediately before we went south was very valuable. Nobody should be sent to fly attack operations in wartime if he has not trained at ultra-low level.

Above and right:
The decisive air attack at Goose Green on the afternoon of 28 May, (*Above***) showing (dotted line) the tracks of Sqn Ldr Peter Harris and Tony Harper attacking with cluster bombs and (dashed line) the track of Sqn Ldr Jerry Pook attacking with rockets. (***Right***) One of the 35mm anti-aircraft guns at Goose Green silenced during the attack; earlier in the day these weapons had been used in the direct fire role against advancing British paratroops.** *No 1 Sqn, Knights*

Below right:
A remarkable shot by the port-facing camera of Flt Lt Mark Hare's GR3, taken during a reconnaissance of Mount London near Port Stanley on 10 June. The Harrier was flying at high speed towards the right of the photograph, as the Argentine soldier on the left struggled to line up and fire his Blowpipe missile launcher at the aircraft. He failed, and Hare knew nothing of the danger until after his return to *Hermes* **and his film was developed.** *MoD*

'Also it is very important to get practice in weapon aiming; there is no point in doing any of the other training, if you cannot get the bombs or rockets on to the target: that is the single most important thing. Almost anybody can get through to a target, but if he cannot put the weapons down accurately he might just as well not have gone.'

Tony Harper feels that the Harrier has come out of its first taste of action showing itself to be a very effective ground - attack aircraft.

'It is a very good aeroplane, it seems to be able to survive battle damage well. Its small size and absence of smoke make it difficult for the enemy to see coming, and the camouflage is effective. It is fast enough at low altitude — if you went much faster you wouldn't have time to pick out the target. It is able to operate from stupidly small strips. It could do with a little more strengthening, armour plating around certain vital components like the fuel system and the pilot'.

Like many a combat pilot before him, Tony Harper found the worst part of the war to be the waiting at cockpit readiness.

'The worst bit of any mission was sitting in the aircraft on deck at 5min cockpit readiness waiting to go, when there was time to worry about what might happen. Once the order came to go it was not so bad, you were too busy to worry. By the end of the conflict all of the squadron pilots were starting to get a bit twitched — it was only a matter of time before somebody got hurt. In the event nobody was, we were bloody lucky nobody on our squadron was killed or seriously injured.

'I expected war to be far more dangerous than it apparently was. And I expected it to be far more spectacular than it was. Beforehand people had said war is 3% sheer panic and 97% boredom, and that is absolutely true.

'Having been to war has made me give a higher value to the more mundane things in life, like taking the dog for a walk or having a beer in the local. I even like mowing the lawn now, I couldn't stand it before I went to the South Atlantic . . .'

Below:
A GR3 of No 1 Squadron about to take off for an attack; note the 1,000lb Paveway laser guided bomb under the port wing, with a normal 1,000-pounder under the starboard wing. *Hare*

Of the band of experienced pilots what went south with the initial wave of No 1 Squadron, Flt Lt Jeff Glover had the least time on the Harrier. Yet even he had more than a year's experience on the aircraft and had previously amassed more than 1,000 hours as an instructor on the Hawk. On 21 May 1982 he took off from HMS Hermes for his first operational mission, to provide air support for British troops going ashore near San Carlos Settlement. The flight was nearly his last. He was shot down, suffered injuries while ejecting from the aircraft, and taken prisoner. After a few days he was airlifted to the mainland and remained in captivity until his release early in July 1982, the only British serviceman to be held in Argentina for any length of time. During his captivity the treatment varied between friendly and hostile, depending on where he was and the course of the war on the Falklands at the time. But he was never physically illtreated, and by February 1983 he had recovered sufficiently to resume flying with No 1 Squadron.

Jeff Glover's first operational mission went sour almost from the beginning. He was to have flown with his squadron commander, Wg Cdr Peter Squire; but after take off the latter's undercarriage failed to retract and he had to return to the ship. Jeff Glover went on alone. When he arrived in the San Carlos area he asked the army forward air controller if there was a target for his cluster bombs. Back came the reply that there appeared to be no Argentine troops in the immediate area. He was asked to fly to Port Howard, 20 miles to the southwest, and attack any enemy positions he found there. The pilot did as he was bid and made a high speed low altitude run northwards over the settlement without seeing anything worth attacking. He informed the controller, and was asked to run past the settlement a second time and photograph it using the Harrier's port-facing camera.

'I climbed to 8,000ft to conserve fuel and stooged around over the centre of West Falkland for about a quarter of an hour, to give a little time for things to quieten down at Port Howard. I wanted to make my second run from a different direction, but there was not a lot of choice because Mount Maria [2,518ft] is immediately to the west of the settlement.

'I decided to run in heading northeast, and that was a mistake because I found myself heading almost straight into the sun. Because of this, I had to concentrate much more on flying the aircraft than watching what was happening outside.'

As the Harrier flew past the east of the settlement, the camera clicking at regular intervals, its pilot again saw nothing of the enemy. The first he knew of their presence was when his aircraft shuddered under the impact of exploding shells — first one, then two more in rapid succession. Almost immediately the Harrier flicked into a violent and uncontrollable roll to the right. Jeff Glover waited until the aircraft had rotated through 320 degrees, then pulled the ejector seat handle.

'After I pulled the handle there was a crash above my head as the explosive charge shattered the canopy, the aircraft was right way up by the time the seat fired. As I was blasted out into the 600mph wind my left arm was wrenched back [although he did not know at the time his left arm, shoulder and collar bone were all broken]. I passed out.

'When I came to I was under water. I worked out which way was "up" and swam to the surface. I came up and saw my parachute floating in the water in front of me.'

Prisoner of the Argentine

Deep in shock, the injured pilot forgot to inflate his life jacket. But fortunately for him there was sufficient air trapped in his rubberised immersion suit to keep him afloat.

'I had a good look around and saw the shore about 200yd away. I started trying to swim towards it on my back but I got nowhere fast — I had not released my parachute harness. So I gave that up and started to think things out. I was in the process of releasing the pack connectors, before inflating my dinghy, when I heard voices and shouts. I looked around and saw about 10 Argentine soldiers standing on the shore. Then a rowing boat put out with half a dozen soldiers on board.

'In the front of the boat was an officer, and under his direction the soldiers came alongside me and hauled me on board; as they lifted me, my arm hurt like hell. The officer spoke to me in good English. He said he was a doctor, asked where it hurt and said I would be all right, he would look after me. One of the things I asked him was "What shot me down?" He said "Everything, we were all firing at you".

'We were rowed to the shore, then we got out of the boat. The officer had a motorbike, I was put on the pillion. The officer drove and we rode off down a rough track, with a soldier on each side jogging along and supporting me. I was holding my left arm with my right, in the most comfortable position I could find. I was bleeding rather a lot from my face, I could see the blood dripping on to the back of the officer's tunic. We continued on the motor bike for about 500 yards, then we arrived at the Port Howard

Below:
Port Howard Settlement, photographed by Sqn Ldr Jerry Pook on 23 May, the day after Flt Lt Jeff Glover was flown out by helicopter. In the middle of the picture, marked with red crosses, is the social centre where the RAF pilot received medical attention after his capture. In the foreground can be seen defensive positions dug by Argentine troops occupying the settlement. *RAF*

social club which the Argentine troops had requisitioned as a medical centre.'

The Argentine officer introduced himself as Marine Captain Santiago Llaños and took personal charge of the prisoner.

'The Captain and the medical orderlies treated me very kindly. I had not been able to look at myself in the mirror, but with the injuries to my face I knew I must have looked a mess. The cuts were probably caused when the explosive cord detonated to shatter the canopy immediately before I ejected, or when my helmet was torn off during the ejection or when I hit the water. My right eye was badly bruised and swollen, I couldn't see out of it.'

At the medical centre the pilot's heavy immersion suit and thick woollen flying underwear were cut away to enable the doctor and orderlies to get at his wounds. The injured arm was bound up and Jeff Glover was dressed in the shapeless jacket and trousers of an Argentine conscript. He remained at the medical centre until the following afternoon, when a Bell UH-1H helicopter arrived to pick him up to fly him to Goose Green.

'While at Port Howard I was the subject of a lot of curiosity, but I did not encounter the slightest hostility. On the way to the helicopter a young Argentine soldier came up to me, the Captain introduced us and said "This is the lad who shot you down, he was in charge of the Blowpipe missile." I said "Good effort!" and shook the man by the hand. That seemed to please him, I had the impression he was worried because I appeared to be badly injured.'

The claim that the Harrier was shot down by a Blowpipe shoulder-launched surface-to-air missile has been widely publicised. But on reflection, and in view of the three explosions he distinctly heard before his aircraft started its final roll, Jeff Glover believes he was shot down by cannon fire from the ground.

The Marine Captain flew with his prisoner to Goose Green where the pair were accommodated in the junior officers' mess, a requisitioned cottage. As at Port Howard, everyone did all they reasonably could for the injured British pilot.

'Some of the young officers were keen to try out their English on me. Several asked if I knew Nick Taylor, the Sea Harrier pilot who had been shot down and killed at Goose Green. When I said I had known him, they expressed sorrow at his death.

'While I was at Goose Green there was no Pucara activity, only the occasional helicopter was flying.'

After a day at Goose Green Jeff Glover and the Marine Captain boarded a helicopter to fly to Port Stanley. The helicopter landed on the racecourse at the western edge of the town, where the doctor bade his captive farewell. The British pilot was handed over to the custody of the Argentine Air Force and taken to the Port Stanley medical centre.

'I was at Port Stanley for about 24 hours. While there I heard anti-aircraft fire at one point, but there was no other action.

'On the night of the 24th I boarded a C-130 Hercules to fly to the mainland. Also on the aircraft were some other wounded, and a few pilots who had ejected from their aircraft. Still everyone was very friendly towards me. On the plane the shot-down pilots tried to strike up a conversation but I did not want to be drawn into it. My big worry was that the Hercules might be intercepted by Sea Harriers and I would be shot down by my own side. But three or four hours later we landed at Commodoro Rivadavia.

'On arrival I was taken to the Air Force hospital. Up till then my arm had been in a sling, now it was put into a plaster cast; the arm gave me some pain, but I was given pain killers. I was put in a ward with my bed partitioned off by curtains. Everybody apart from the doctors and medical orderlies wore pistol holsters, but it soon became clear that these were because there was a war on and not because I was there. The food was not brilliant, I got the same fare as the Argentine conscripts. Most people were very kind to me and wanted to try out their English, though I did get the odd scowl. I could get no information at all on the course of the war, or whether or not the British landings had succeeded.'

Now nearly a week into his captivity, Jeff Glover began to wonder when somebody was going to get around to interrogating him: all Royal Air Force aircrew receive training in how to behave in such a situation, but the injured pilot was in no state to resist if undue force was used.

'At Commodoro Rivadavia this very smooth guy came in for a chat, it was immediately obvious what he was after. He introduced himself in perfect English and tried to strike up a conversation. His first words were "I expect you would like to speak to somebody in English, wouldn't you?" At the time I wasn't fussed, I was feeling pretty drowsy from the pain killers. He started talking about travel. I did not say much, I just answered yes and no, the minimum that politeness demanded. He came to see me each day and kept trying to bring the conversation around to military matters. But he never got anywhere and in the end he gave up coming.

'After a few days in the hospital I was moved to the Officers' Mess at Commodore Rivadavia, I was kept in a room with an armed corporal outside the door. On about a dozen occasions individual officers came in to chat to me. They were just being friendly, there was no attempt to grill me on military matters. On one occasion a Learjet pilot brought me a bottle of wine. Another visitor was not so friendly. He came into the room and looked at me, then said "I don't like what you British are doing, but because you are a Harrier pilot I will shake your hand." We shook hands, I asked him what he flew and he said "Mirages". Then he walked out.'

Early in June Jeff Glover was flown to Chamical air base in La Rioja province in the north of Argentina, to face the most difficult phase of imprisonment.
'At Chamical none of the officers made friendly visits and I could detect more hostility in the atmosphere. For about a week I was kept in a shuttered room with an adjoining bathroom in the Officers' Mess. The food was poor and I was permitted only two hot drinks per day. After a week they allowed me to use a small courtyard for exercise, for an hour each day. I began to get the feeling that something had gone very wrong for Argentina: either she had lost the World Cup or the war — or perhaps both!"

While at Chamical Jeff Glover received two visits from the Swiss Red Cross, and early in July he learned that he was to be repatriated. On the 6th he was flown to Buenos Aires and taken to the main Air Force hospital, where the plaster cast was removed from his arm. He spent two nights there. Then on the 8th he was flown to Montevideo in an Argentine Air Force transport and handed over to the Uraguayan authorities.
'A car arrived from the British embassy, and I was taken to the ambassador's residence.

For the first time in nearly seven weeks I could unwind, talk freely and enjoy a few gins.
'The next day I boarded a British Caledonian DC-10 for the flight back to England. When we arrived at Gatwick my wife Dee was allowed up the steps and into the aircraft to meet me. She gave me a super hug but my arm had been in plaster for 42 days, it was locked and quite painful. I had to say to her "Take it easy!" '

Jeff Glover has no hard feelings towards the Argentinians he encountered during his captivity. During the first part of his confinement his treatment was never less than correct and at times it was very friendly. For the last five weeks things were more difficult, but he was never physically illtreated. Given the range of misfortunes that can befall a prisoner of war, he had got off very lightly.
'I met some nice people who were very kind to me and I should like to meet them again if I have the chance. The attitudes of those around me altered to mild hostility at the time of the surrender, but I was never badly treated. I do hope nothing happened to Captain Santiago Laños during the later fighting on the Falklands, he had been particularly kind to me.'

Below:
10 July 1982: accompanied by his wife Dee, Jeff Glover seen on his arrival at Gatwick after returning from captivity in Argentina.

One of the many Harrier modifications crash-produced for the Falklands conflict was the self-protection jammer unofficially nicknamed 'Blue Eric' after its project officer, Sqn Ldr Eric Annal. During the conflict he was working at the Ministry of Defence in Whitehall, in the section concerned with service requirements for new electronic warfare equipment. Under the pressure of war the 'Blue Eric' jammer went from its initial concept to 10 examples built, tested and ready to move south, in the almost unbelievably short time of only fifteen days. It was an interesting piece of engineering and in this account Eric Annal, an electronic engineer himself, tells how it was done.

'On 6 May 1982 my boss at MoD, Wg Cdr Malcolm Caygill, outlined the requirement for a self-protection jammer for the Harrier. We got together with the people at the Operations Branch at MoD to determine which enemy threat radars they were most concerned about.'

Once the decision had been taken on which enemy radars the Harriers would need to be able to counter, Eric Annal had to determine which of these could in fact be countered with the sort of jammer that could be produced rapidly. For this, he was able to call in assistance from the electronic warfare department at Farnborough, and the Royal Air Force's Electronic Warfare Operational Support Establishment (EWOSE) at Benson which provided detailed information on the characteristics of the types of radars used by the Argentine forces.

'I phoned Marconi Space and Defence Systems at Stanmore and said I would be up to see them that afternoon. I had dealt with them a lot before, they were our main contractor. Either they could do what we wanted, or nobody could. I arranged for representatives from Farnborough and EWOSE to be at the meeting also. There were about 10 of us, with Bryan Sheppard leading the MSDS team.

'We looked at the MSDS "Sky Shadow" jamming pod on the Tornado, and the American Westinghouse ALQ-101 pod used on the Buccaneer; but these were both too big and too heavy to go on the Harrier. The next thought was to take part of the Sky Shadow electronics and put it in a shorter and lighter pod; but that would have taken up one of the weapons stations on the Harrier — and there were few enough of those anyway. As an alternative it was suggested that we put some of the Sky Shadow electronics into one of the gun pods on the Harrier, and we agreed to look into the possibility of doing that.

'By Friday, 7 May, we were looking at the feasibility of the two alternatives: the reduced capability Sky Shadow in a smaller under-wing pod or in a modified gun pod. We started doing sums to see what the implications would be regarding power supplies, cooling requirements, etc.'

At this stage Eric Annal was joined by Flt Lt Bob Munns, an RAF engineering officer attached to Marconi, who became No 2 on the project. By now there was less interest in the underwing jamming pod for the jammer and this was dropped in favour of the modified gun pod.

'On Saturday 8th Bob and I went to the British Aerospace works at Kingston to see about the implications of fitting a jammer into a gun pod. There we dealt with George Latham, the expert on the Harrier electrical system. He said we would be able to get the power we wanted from the snatch connector which normally plugs into the aircraft's reconnaissance pod when it is fitted.

'While we were there the company was looking into the possibility of fitting the ALE-40 chaff and infra-red decoy dispenser into the Harrier. That was Harrier modification No 1500, mine became No 1504.'

On the following day Annal and Munns journeyed up to Wittering to look over a Harrier and discuss the operational implications of fitting the jammer into the pod. By the following morning — only five days after the initial discussions — Marconi had completed design work on the gun-pod jammer.

'On Monday, 10th, MSDS started putting the prototype jammer together. Most of the components came from Sky Shadow, the rest were bought off the shelf or specially manufactured; at the same time the electronics had to be completely repackaged to fit in the gun pod. From the beginning H. R. Smith Ltd, who make radomes, were in the picture. They designed and built the special fibreglass radomes we needed and delivered a set on Tuesday 11th.'

By Wednesday 12th, seven days after the start, the prototype 'Blue Eric' was complete and ready for ground testing:

'We put the pod on the vibrating table at MSDS and gave it 25min at 3g, then 5min at 14g. Initially there were some problems, like

screws starting to wind themselves out. These had to be wire-locked in. But apart from that the electronics survived the ordeal quite well.

'Another problem was how to cool this jammer, the power source produced quite a bit of heat. Normally we would have used a proper glycol cooling system but there was no time to design and build that. In the end we had a block of copper machined with fins to carry away the heat, using air ducted in from the normal intake scoop fitted to the gun pod. When the equipment was run on the ground, with no ram-air cooling, we imposed a maximum time on transmit of 2min.'

On 14 May 'Blue Eric' flew for the first time, fitted to a Harrier piloted by Flt Lt Steve Cheeseman. But shortly after the jamming pod was switched to transmit, it failed. This caused some worries to those who had built 'Blue Eric' but the cause was nothing more serious that a blown fuse in the electrical supply circuit. After checking with British Aerospace that the wiring would take the heavier load, a fuse of higher rating was fitted in its place and this cured the problem.

On the next day, Saturday 15th, the jamming pod was flown again. The Harrier went out to Wainfleet and fired off a full magazine of ammunition from the port 30mm Aden gun pod immediately adjacent to the pod carrying Blue Eric. The vibration produced no problems and after the firing the jammer worked perfectly. The trial demonstrated that 'Blue Eric' could live next to a gun pod, now the question was whether the gun pod — with a magazine full of electrically fired 30mm rounds — could live safely next to the jammer. There was a chance, albeit a small one, that the radiated energy from the jammer might be sufficient to fire the cartridges of the 30mm rounds and thus give rise to a highly dangerous situation. A specially instrumented gun pack was fitted and the transmitter run to see if there was any such danger. There was none, and on the following day 'Blue Eric' was pronounced safe for operational use. The jammer was now cleared to undergo full air testing against special ground receivers in position at a Royal Air Force electronic warfare test range.

On Tuesday 18th production of the batch of 10 'Blue Eric' pods was started, as Eric Annal described:

'We stripped out the gun pods, always bearing in mind that they might have to be returned to use as gun pods. The electronics for the jammer went into the centre section, with a waveguide running to the front end. The rear section, where the ammunition magazine was situated, was left empty; that space we could have used had there been a later need to enhance the capability of the equipment. There were about 30 people at Marconi involved in putting the "Blue Eric" pods together. The firm was magnificent. We were in a wartime situation, with everyone pulling together.'

Four days after production started, the initial batch was complete and nine 'Blue Eric' pods left Stanmore for Wittering for installation on Harriers; the remaining jamming pod was held at the company to serve as a reference model. From the initial conception of the jammer, to delivery of nine production pods, had taken only 15 days.

Below:
In addition to 'Blue Eric' the four GR3s flown direct to *Hermes* (two on 1 June and two on 8 June) each carried two ALE-40 dispensers, for Chaff and infra-red decoy flares, recessed into the fuselage immediately behind the airbrake. *Author*

The jamming pods were fitted to the second batch of Harriers being prepared at Wittering to go south, at the same time as these aircraft were being adapted to carry the ALE-40 chaff and infra-red decoy flare dispensers. On 28 May the first aircraft of this batch took off from Wittering to fly to Ascension; and on 1 June Flt Lts Murdo Macleod and Mike Beech took off from Ascension for the monumental 8hr 25min flights, with no land diversions along almost the entire route, and landed on HMS *Hermes*. A further two Harriers with 'Blue Eric' followed them to the carrier on 8 June.

After all the effort that had gone into producing the jamming pods, it would be nice to be able to say they had an influence on the fighting. But this was not to be. Following the arrival of the first two modified Harriers there were four days of very bad weather over the Falklands which precluded ground-attack operations. When the Harriers did resume flying the land fighting was in its final phase and the aircraft were sent mainly against Argentine positions near the front line, clear of targets defended by the types of radar the jammer had been designed to counter. In the event, 'Blue Eric' was never used in action.

So was the production of 'Blue Eric' worthwhile? The answer has to be 'yes'. Had the Argentine ground forces put up a stiffer fight than they did, and Harriers had to go into action against targets defended by the radars the jammer was intended to counter, then 'Blue Eric' might have seen considerable use. Both the Royal Air Force and industry learned a great deal about how modern electronic countermeasures equipment can be produced very rapidly and this knowledge could stand them in good stead in the future. Although during the Falklands Conflict foreign companies proved very helpful, it would be unrealistic to expect that such assistance will automatically be forthcoming in any future conflict. 'Blue Eric', and other crash-programmes carried through during the conflict, have demonstrated the vital importance of a strong indigenous defence industry in time of national crisis.

At the end of the Falklands Conflict 'Blue Eric' did not die; at the time of writing the electronics from some of these pods is in use at Farnborough for a special development trial. And if the need should arise, the project could be quickly resurrected.

The cost of the 'Blue Eric' programme was about £500,000, with everyone working flat-out. How would that have compared with a programme to produce a similar jammer in normal times? Are crash-programmes an expensive way of producing military equipment? Eric Annal replied:

'In the normal way, this contract could have taken about two years and cost £2million. So it would have cost four times as much. Would such a jammer have been better than "Blue Eric"? Yes. Would it have been four times better? Probably no.

'Even when a company has guys working on a crash project day and night on overtime, there is a limit to the number of man hours that can be charged to it. As one well-known company director later commented about some aspects of his firm's work during the Falklands Conflict, "If you take only 15 days to do a job, there is a limit to how much you can charge for it . . . .'

'Wild Weasel' Harrier. Another of the modifications rapidly introduced for use in the Falklands conflict was the fitting of Shrike radiation homing missiles and their associated firing equipment into the Harrier, for attacks on enemy ground radars. One GR3 on *Hermes* was modified to carry Shrike, but the work was completed too late for the missile to be used in action.

Currently serving on the Strike Command Briefing Team, Wg Cdr Peter Squire joined the Royal Air Force in 1963 and served three years as an officer cadet at Cranwell. His first operational tour was with No 20 Squadron at Singapore, flying Hunters in the day fighter and ground attack roles; he then became an instructor on the Hunter, spent a brief period with the Red Arrows aerobatic team, then went to Germany where he served on a Harrier squadron. In 1980 he was posted to a staff appointment at Headquarters Strike Command, then in March 1981 he resumed flying Harriers when he took command of No 1 Squadron at Wittering. During the Falklands conflict he led the squadron into action, for which he received the Distinguished Flying Cross. With his long experience in the attack role and as the only man to command a Harrier GR3 squadron in action, Peter Squire is uniquely qualified to discuss the relevance of the Falklands experience to any future conflict in Central Europe. In this account he goes on to give an insight into the nature of ground attack operations by the Harrier and the sort of ground-attack aircraft he thinks the Royal Air Force should be considering as a replacement for the AV-8B/Harrier GR5. He begins with an overview of Harrier ground attack operations during the Falklands conflict and says how he thinks they differed from the sort of operations the aircraft would undertake in any conflict in Central Europe.

'The flying was pretty much what we had trained for except that instead of keeping low the whole time, as we would expect to have to during operations over Central Europe, range considerations dictated that we had to fly from the carrier to the islands at high altitude, go down to attack, then climb back to high altitude to return to the carrier. During the high altitude transits we never saw another aircraft apart from the odd Sea Harrier on its way out or back. So the first and the last half hour of each sortie was very peaceful and almost unreal. We would let down to low altitude and still not see any enemy aircraft. In fact nobody on the squadron saw an Argentine fixed-wing aircraft airborne, ever. We would not expect things to be so easy in any conflict over Central Europe.

'Over the Falklands it was relatively easy to fly very low because there were virtually no obstructions, high tension cables, trees, etc. The only man-made obstructions are in the immediate vicinity of Port Stanley town where there are some high wireless aerials. The other thing that helped was that over the Falklands navigation at low level was very easy: there are few settlements and they and the coastal features and hills are all distinctive and easy to recognise. If a pilot is happy that he knows where he is, he will be prepared to fly a lot lower. Once a pilot becomes uncertain of his position he will climb, because he has to concentrate more on navigating than on flying low. Also, when he flew over the Falklands, by and large the weather was good. Either there was very good visibility at low altitude, with an acceptable cloud base with perhaps the odd shower that you could steer yourself around; or it was so bad that you really couldn't fly at all. There were very few days when we had to force on in bad weather with the visibility below a couple of miles and cloud base below 200ft. None of those characteristics apply to the central region of Europe. There you have a lot of high tension cables, villages with church spires which go up quite high, and an enormous number of woods. These will force the pilot of an attack aircraft to fly higher than he would like. Another major problem is industrial haze, always present over parts of

The Harrier as a Ground Attack Aircraft

central Europe, which reduces horizontal visibility even on an otherwise clear day. Moreover, in central Europe there are far fewer distinctive features so navigation is much more difficult. Pilots will not be so confident of their position and this will tend to force them to fly higher.'

The Falklands conflict underlined the importance of realistic training, which enabled the heavily outnumbered force of Harriers and Sea Harriers to maintain air superiority over the islands.

'I think our system of training, and the way we go about our training in peacetime, are second to none. I think whatever air force you look at, you would find that our pilots are trained as well, if not better. Our aeroplanes were different from those of the Argentinians, but they weren't that much more sophisticated in terms of the equipment they had on board; and in some aspects they were less sophisticated. So the difference was the training of our pilots. On the Sea Harrier side it was good training combined with a very effective air-to-air missile.'

When operating in the ground-attack role, Harrier pilots have a laid-down set of tactics for use in most eventualities. Peter Squire feels there is nothing wrong with flying this sort of operation 'by the book', provided 'the book' has been carefully thought out and pilots are flexible enough to think out their own tactics if the standard procedures do not apply. His comments, though related to Harrier operations, are in many cases applicable to close air support and battlefield interdiction missions by other types of aircraft.

'On the tactical side I think it is important for an attack squadron to have recognised standard operating procedures for a variety of different eventualities, which will stand you in good stead on most occasions. With the Harrier the RAF operates a system of in-cockpit tasking, where the pilot stays in the cockpit between sorties. That makes it important to have standard procedures which reduce the need for complicated briefings cockpit to cockpit. But you must accept that the standard procedures will not always apply. You might have to change the tactics, in terms of the formations flown or the response made to an unexpected situation. You should never get so blinkered that you cannot see that every now and again you will have to do something totally different.

'Normally the RAF flies the Harrier in a basic two-ship attack formation, though we have a variety of formations we can fly depending on whether the air-to-air threat is greater than the ground-to-air threat, or vice versa, and the ease of finding the target. Operating with a four-ship formation, the procedures will be slightly more complicated. Then you superimpose on these procedures the tactics a formation will adopt to a threat from enemy fighters or ground-launched missiles or guns. We pre-plan the order in which aircraft attack, and the attack profile depending on the type of weapon to be used: bombs, rockets or cannon. Then we pre-plan the procedure to be adopted after leaving the target: should we all run out hell-for-leather as fast as we can as individuals, if the main threat is from ground fire; or should we regroup and try and give each other mutual support in case we are attacked by enemy fighters. So we do think about it in quite a lot of detail, and we do have standard procedures for most situations. But if the situation facing you does not match any of these you don't say, "We'll do that anyway"; you re-think the tactics and adapt the procedures to the new situation.'

The route to and from the target would be carefully chosen to avoid, wherever possible, all known or likely defended areas. But enemy fighters may try to engage at any time, and modern battlefield anti-aircraft systems are highly mobile; so the pilots of attack aircraft have to be continually on the alert to detect the first signs of any attempt by the enemy to engage with fighters or

surface weapons. Peter Squire described in general terms how a formation of attack aircraft would react to such threats, once they have been detected. First he considers the threat from fighters.

'Ideally we don't want to have to react too much on the way to the target, because that may jeopardise our chances of getting there. In a series of turns we might use too much fuel or, in the last resort, we might have to jettison our bombs or rockets to save our skins. In either case we would not hit our intended target. So our primary objective is to try and avoid an engagement if at all possible. If threatened by enemy fighters we would go as fast as we can, to make it more difficult for them to catch us. At the same time we would reduce altitude and try to lose ourselves in the environment over which we were flying. If we can use the terrain — for example if there is a valley we can fly down hugging the ground, while going fast so that the rate of closure of the enemy fighters is less, we may be able to escape without their even seeing us. Of, if they have seen us, they may lose contact. One thing helping us in this is the fact that low down the Harrier is difficult to see; it is a small aeroplane with a smoke-free engine, and its camouflage is very effective. If these measures fail, then we would have to try and defeat a missile of gun attack by the enemy fighters.'

Flying in the standard Royal Air Force battle formation, a pilot under attack from an enemy fighter would immediately receive support from one or more of his comrades. Usually the threat of an aircraft swinging in behind will be sufficient to force an enemy pilot to break away — only a very brave, or a very foolhardy, man would press home an attack when he knows he has an enemy aircraft on his tail. Peter Squire then went on to discuss the Harrier's ability to use VIFF (thrust Vectored In Forward Flight) during air-to-air combat at low altitude; in his view pilots should use this tactic only with great care.

'I think that VIFFing should never be an automatic reaction during air-to-air combat. Used at the right time, it can give one an advantage. For example, if you see an enemy fighter closing rapidly from the stern quarter and he is outside missile range but only just, then by suddenly slowing down you could force him to close to below the minimum range to launch a missile. But VIFFing used at the wrong time could put one at a disadvantage. If, for example, you are being attacked by an enemy fighter and you use VIFF to slow down to stay outside his missile firing bracket or force him to overshoot, if he has somebody in trail by two or three miles coming in from the other side in a pincer movement, you then become a stationary target for the No 2 and really easy meat. So I think the use of VIFF must never be automatic, nor regarded as the be all and end all. It is a capability the aircraft has which does have its good points, but it can also put one into a dangerous situation if it used unwisely.'

One interesting point that came out of the Falklands conflict was that Argentine pilots were most reluctant to engage in close combat with Harriers or Sea Harriers, at any altitude, because they knew VIFFing would enable the enemy aircraft to behave in an unpredictable way. For fighter pilots who have not had the chance to train against the Harrier, and hopefully this would be so for those who would engage it in war, the uncertainty of engaging a VIFF-capable aircraft for the first time in combat is a daunting prospect.

'The Harrier is quite good at low speed and low altitude in a one-versus-one combat. But we can do little against a faster aircraft if it refuses ever to slow down — which is what a fighter that cannot fight a low-speed combat

ought to do. If the enemy pilot carries out a series of high speed passes and, if he doesn't get into a firing position, he goes around again until he does or runs short of fuel and has to go home, then the faster aircraft ought never to lose. The trouble is that fighter pilots, being proud people, tend to get sucked into a low-speed fight. They think "I can beat him!", they slow down to pull a turn tighter, and if they do that the Harrier will get them. Obviously, if the Harrier is carrying Sidewinder missiles and can get a shot at the enemy even if it has the advantage of speed, that becomes much more of an even fight.'

Peter Squire believes that a proportion of the attack aircraft in any large force should carry air-to-air missiles, if they are sent against targets likely to be defended by fighters. In that case the enemy pilots would have to regard any attack aircraft seen as likely to be missile-armed, and would be much more careful about engaging. This, in turn, would make it easier for the attack aircraft to escape even if they have been intercepted. When operating in their normal attack role Harrier pilots will regard an inconclusive combat with no kill on either side as a satisfactory outcome: their aim is to hit ground targets and survive to go back again, not slug it out with the opposing fighter force.

If the enemy fighter manages to get into a firing position and launches a missile at a Harrier, the combat is still far from lost. Air-to-air missiles come in two types, infra-red homing and radar semi-active, and the Harriers have standard procedures to deal with either type.

'Since it is fitted with a fan-jet engine, the infra-red signature of the Harrier is smaller than that of most comparable attack aircraft, and it is much smaller than that of an aircraft using afterburner. Also, because the Harrier's jet pipes are underneath the wings, they are partially masked to a missile coming from above or from the side. If you turn towards an opposing fighter, the normal counter to any attack, you put your wing between him and the heat source and so further reduce the amount of infra-red energy radiated in his direction. So the basic configuration of the aircraft makes it a poor infra-red target. If at the same time you deflect the nozzles, that further reduces the infra-red signature of the Harrier. You do not need to reduce the infra-red signature of the aircraft by much if you can introduce another heat source, such as an infra-red decoy flare, for the missile to go after.

'If the threat is from a radar-guided missile there will be a period of warning from the Harrier's radar warning receiver; then one has to try to break the radar lock-on, either

Scenes at Port Stanley after No 1 Squadron went ashore to provide air defence for the islands. (*Top*) **Carrying a couple of Sidewinder missiles, a GR3 sits at the end of the runway at Port Stanley connected to a Unimog truck. Note the rocky surrounds.** (*Above*) **One of the Harriers on QRA (Quick Reaction Alert), with the pilots on readiness in the hut nearby.**

If engaged by enemy surface-to-air weapons systems, missiles or guns, the attack aircraft have a set of tactics to cover each type of threat.

'If you are some miles from the target and your radar warning receiver picks up signals from, say, a surface-to-air missile battery in your path, if you have sufficient fuel you can turn away to pass clear of it to one side. When the threat has passed, you can resume the planned route. If you are within a few seconds of weapon release you are probably better off carrying on, mentally putting blinkers on and going for the target.

'If they are launched in your direction, surface-launched infra-red homing missiles can be countered in the same way as air-launched weapons.

'If the threat is a radar-controlled surface-to-air missile or gun battery, there will usually be some indication on the aircraft's radar warning receiver of the type of weapon and its relative bearing. We would then fly as fast as we could to reduce the time spent within range of the enemy system, fly as low as possible to try and go below the minimum engagement altitude of that particular system, and try to put something — a hill or some trees — between us and the launching site or gun battery to negate the threat.'

The release of chaff, co-ordinated with a manoeuvre and low flying, will usually break a lock-on from a surface fire-control radar. Optically sighted anti-aircraft guns are far less accurate than radar-laid weapons, and are best countered by flying fast and low and trying to hide behind whatever cover is available. Light machine gun or rifle fire is almost

by flying close to the ground, manoeuvring, releasing chaff or a combination of all three.'

Another very effective counter to an attack with this type of missile, if the Harrier under attack is part of a formation, is if the other aircraft can move into position to threaten the attacking fighter. To engage with a radar semi-active missile, the attacker must keep his radar locked-on to the target aircraft from some time before launch until the missile reaches the target. During this time the attacking fighter cannot manoevure violently, and is itself vulnerable to attack; if it can be forced to evade and break the radar lock-on, the missile will cease to guide and will almost certainly miss its target.

Harrier pilots regard a fighter attack with guns as the easiest threat to deal with. If the enemy pilot decides to fight on their terms, comes down to low altitude and reduces speed to try to bring his gunsight to bear, he could be in for a nasty surprise . . .

(*Left*) **During a gale in August 1982 the frame of one of the canvas hangars at Port Stanley collapsed on the Harrier inside, causing serious damage.** (*Below*) **XZ889, which suffered serious damage on 8 June after a partial engine failure as it was about to land at the San Carlos airstrip, being brought to Port Stanley airfield under a Chinook of No 18 Squadron.**
MoD, Robertshaw

impossible to avoid, because an attack aircraft might be engaged by such weapons at any time while over hostile territory. Usually they fire non-tracer ammunition, so unless the pilot sees the muzzle flashes or his aircraft is hit, there is no indication that he is being fired at. Fortunately for the pilots, however, this type of fire is the least accurate of all; and during the Falklands conflict attack aircraft on both sides showed that they could take several hits from small arms and still return to base. When faced with this type of fire, an attack pilot can only grit his teeth and press on.

'If you approach an attack with determination, then usually you will come out OK. It is a bit like a rugby tackle: if you go into it shying away, you stand a much greater chance of getting hurt.'

Having reached the target, everything will have been in vain if the bombs, rockets or cannon shells miss the target, or hit it but fail

to inflict serious damage. So it is extremely important that the pilots are trained to attack accurately, and receive constant practice to maintain their skill.

'The Harrier is predominantly a close support aeroplane, with weapons designed specifically to knock out enemy tanks; and these are very small, hard targets. And even though the cluster bombs or rockets we use are, to a degree, area weapons, you still have to be pretty accurate to score a hit. You can't afford to be a long way out. And if you miss, you have put your aeroplane and yourself in jeopardy for nothing.'

During the operations by No 1 Squadron over the Falklands, two out of the three Harriers shot down were hit when their pilots returned to the target soon after the initial attack, in order to make a second. This raises the thorny question of the second-pass attack — is it ever worth the risk?

'I would say the second pass is about twice as dangerous as the first pass, depending on the strength of the defences around the target. If the target is not well defended, obviously one can attack it again without undue risk. But if there are defences and they have been alerted, the decision on whether to re-attack depends on what has been found in the target area. If there is a very lucrative target, then I believe that if you miss it the first time you have to have another stab — particularly if it is a mobile target that is not going to be there in an hour. Certainly I don't think one can lay down a hard and fast rule that says one should never go back to the same target for a second pass. That must depend on the situation on the ground and the importance of that target to our own forces and those of the enemy.'

As an example of the sort of lucrative target that warrants a re-attack, Peter Squire cited the action by Sqn Ldr Jerry Pook and Flt Lt Mark Hare at dawn on 21 May 1982, after the pair came upon four Argentine helicopters, a Chinook, two Pumas and a Bell UH-1, on the grond near Mount Kent. In the half light the two pilots made repeated attack runs on the helicopters with cluster bombs and cannon, until Hare's GR3 was hit by ground fire and the pair were forced to break away. The Chinook and the two Pumas were destroyed, considerably reducing the Argentine helicopter lifting capacity on the Falklands.

'A group of three or four helicopters was a sizeable proportion of the number available to the Argentine forces on the islands. They had to supply their various garrisons by helicopter because they couldn't do it by road. So those helicopters were a highly lucrative target and I would certainly have gone round again to make sure of getting as many as possible. Nobody wants to get shot down, nobody wants to sacrifice his life. But in war, every now and again, your have to take risks; you will not win unless you do. And the proof of the pudding was that both Harriers did get back, with only minor damage to one of them.'

Having given an overview of Harrier ground-attack operations, what sort of aircraft would Peter Squire expect to see replacing the AV-8B and Harrier GR5 in this role?

'Assuming we would still have manned aeroplanes for this role, and I do, then I think we would still want to have a mix of aeroplanes; a longer range, highly sophisticated two-seater type to replace the present Tornado; and a relatively simple shorter range type with a short take off and vertical landing (STOVL) capability to replace the Harrier. I think it would be unwise to put all of our eggs in one basket, to try to carry out both roles with the same type of aircraft — I don't think there is any merit in using a very expensive aeroplane like the Tornado replacement to do the close air support and battlefield air interdiction roles which the far cheaper Harrier replacement would be able to do. That would be like using a sledgehammer to crack a nut. Also you need at least two types of aircraft, one which will need runways and one which will not. This will greatly complicate the problem of an opposing air force trying to deny us the use of our airfields.

'I think the short range attack aircraft, the Harrier replacement, should have a supersonic dash capability — up to about Mach 1.3 for a short time, so that it can escape when attacked. It should be able to take off with only a small run, about 400yd, with its full fuel and weapons load; and it should be able to land vertically at the end of the sortie. I do not think it necessary for the aircraft to be able to take off vertically with a full load.'

Peter Squire laid great importance on fitting a really good navigation and weapon aiming system to a future ground-attack aircraft.

'If you can halve the weapon aiming errors, you can inflict the same amount of damage on the enemy with one quarter the number of aircraft; or you can inflict four times the amount of damage with the same number of aircraft. So it is worth spending a lot of money on a good system for weapon aiming.'

He thinks the main anti-tank weapons for such an attack aircraft should be developed versions of the present-day cluster bomb or armour-piercing rocket, rather than a large anti-tank cannon as fitted to the A-10 Thunderbolt.

'You could put a large cannon in a pod on an aircraft like the AV-8B or Harrier GR5. But I am not a fan of that type of weapon. During a battle in central Europe I don't think it will be possible for the pilot of a fast attack aircraft to fire his cannon at its maximum range, because of the difficulty of finding and lining up on an enemy tank at that distance when there is smoke or industrial haze. The pilot would have to go in a lot closer to the target, the length of the firing burst is going to be very short before he has to break away. Also you have to be extraordinarily accurate with a weapon like that: if your rounds miss a tank by just one foot, you have missed it altogether. You would be better off with an area weapon like a pod of rockets.

'The cannon is a great weapon in the A-10, because the aeroplane flies so slowly. But in action I would not particularly want to be flying an aeroplane which attacks at the speed they are going to. Due to the reduced ranges at which they are going to pick up their targets, I think the A-10 pilots are going to have to go in much closer than they would like — over central Europe it is not going to be as it was over Southeast Asia, where for much of the time there is almost unlimited visibility and an attacking aircraft could stand off a long way and attack from there.'

Left:
The next step in the Harrier story: the AV-8B to be co-produced by McDonnell Douglas and British Aerospace. This version features a redesigned wing and tail, Sea Harrier-type canopy and numerous smaller improvements which, together, greatly increase the aircraft's range and offensive load carrying ability especially in the vertical take-off and landing modes of operation. At the time of writing orders for this version include 336 for the US Marine Corps (plus four development aircraft, the first and second of which are seen here) and 60 for the Royal Air Force (as the Harrier GR5).

115

Argentine Aircraft Destroyed by Harriers and Sea Harriers during the Falklands Conflict, May-June 1982

Unless otherwise stated, aircraft were destroyed by Sea Harriers

	Date	Time (local)	Type and unit	Details
1	1 May	08.15	Islander	Destroyed on the ground by cluster bombs from Sea Harrier of No 800 Sqn during attack on Port Stanley airfield. Claimed by Flt Lt Dave Morgan.
2	1 May	08.20	Pucara Grupo 3	Destroyed on the ground by cluster bomb from Sea Harrier of No 800 Sqn during attack on Goose Green Airfield.
3	1 May	16.30	Mirage Grupo 8	Shot down by Sidewinder by Flt Lt Paul Barton of No 801 Sqn, north of West Falkland. Lt Perona ejected.
4	1 May	16.31	Mirage Grupo 8	Severely damaged by Sidewinder by Lt Steve Thomas of No 801 Sqn, north of West Falkland. Attempting an emergency landing at Port Stanley Airfield, aircraft engaged by Argentine anti-aircraft fire. Capt Cuerva killed. Credited to Lt Thomas because even if the Mirage had landed, it would probably never have been able to take off again.
5	1 May	16.41	Dagger Grupo 6	Shot down by Sidewinder by Flt Lt Tony Penfold of No 800 Sqn over West Falkland. Lt Ardiles killed.
6	1 May	16.45	Canberra Grupo 2	Shot down by Sidewinder by Lt Curtiss of No 801 Sqn NW of Falklands. Lt Gonzales and Lt Ibanez killed.
7	21 May	08.15	Chinook Army	Destroyed on the ground by 30mm cannon by Flt Lt Mark Hare in a Harrier GR3 of No 1 Sqn, on Mount Kent.
8	21 May	08.15	Puma Army	As above.
9	21 May	08.15	Puma Army	Destroyed on the ground by above and Sqn Ldr Jerry Pook, No 1 Sqn.
10	21 May	12.10	Pucara Grupo 3	Shot down by 30mm cannon by Lt Cdr 'Sharkey' Ward of No 800 Sqn, near Goose Green. Maj Tomba ejected.
11, 12	21 May	13.04	2×Skyhawk Grupo 4	Shot down by Sidewinders by Lt-Cdr Mike Blissett and Lt-Cdr Neil Thomas of No 800 Sqn near Chartres, West Falkland. Lts Lopez and Manzotti killed.

Appendices

	Date	Time (local)	Type and unit	Details
13	21 May	14.20	Dagger Grupo 6	Shot down by Sidewinder by Lt-Cdr 'Fred' Frederiksen of No 800 Sqn SE of Mount Robinson, West Falkland. Lt Luna ejected.
14, 15, 16	21 May	14.53	3 × Dagger Grupo 6	Shot down by Sidewinders by Lt-Cdr 'Sharkey' Ward (1) and Lt Steve Thomas (2) of No 801 Sqn N of Port Howard, West Falkland. Maj Piuma, Capt Donadille and Lt Senn ejected.
17	21 May	15.11	Skyhawk 3rd Nav Ftr & Attack Escuadrilla	Shot down by Sidewinder by Lt Clive Morell of No 800 Sqn, over Falkland Sound. Lt-Cdr Philippi ejected.
18	21 May	15.11	As above	Shot down by 30mm cannon by Flt Lt John Leeming of No 800 Sqn, over Falkland Sound. Lt Marquez killed.
19	21 May	15.21	As above	Damaged by small arms fire while attacking HMS *Ardent*, suffered further damage from 30mm cannon fire by Lt Morell of No 800 Sqn, over Falkland Sound. Tried to make emergency landing at Port Stanley Airfield but undercarriage could not be lowered. Lt Arca ejected.
20	23 May	10.15	Puma Army	Flew into the ground while attempting to avoid attack by Flt Lt Morgan of No 800 Sqn, near Shag Cove.
21	23 May	10.16	Agusta 109 Army	Shot up on the ground by 30mm cannon by Flt Lts Morgan and Leeming of No 800 Sqn near Shag Cove.
22	23 May	10.16	Puma Army	Shot up on the ground by 30mm cannon by Flt Lt Morgan of No 800 Sqn and Lt-Cdrs Gedge and Braithwaite of No 801 Sqn, near Shag Cove.
23	23 May	16.00	Dagger Grupo 6	Shot down by Sidewinder by Lt Martin Hale of No 800 Sqn over Pebble Island. Lt Volponi killed.
24, 25, 26	24 May	11.00	3 × Dagger Grupo 6	Shot down by Sidewinders fired by Lt-Cdr Andy Auld (2) and Lt Dave Smith (1) of No 800 Sqn over Pebble Island. Major Puga and Capt Diaz ejected, Lt Castillo killed.
27	26 May	15.10	Puma Army	Shot up on the ground by 30mm cannon by Sqn Ldr Pook of No 1 Sqn, on Mount Kent.
28	1 June	10.50	C-130 Hercules Grupo 1	Shot down by Sidewinder and 30mm cannon by Lt-Cdr 'Sharkey' Ward of No 801 Sqn, north of San Carlos Water. Capt Krause and six crew killed.
29, 30, 31	8 June	16.47	3 × Skyhawk Grupo 5	Shot down by Sidewinders fired by Flt Lt Dave Morgan (2) and Lt Dave Smith (1) of No 800 Sqn over Choiseul Sound. Lt Arraras, Lt Bolzan and Ensign Vazquez killed.

NB: After the conflict several Argentine aircraft were captured after having been damaged beyond repair during air attacks and/or surface bombardment from ships; in some cases the damage was cumulative. Where it has not been possible to establish with certainty the cause of the irreparable damage, the aircraft has been omitted from the above list.

The information given comes from *Air War South Atlantic* by Jeffrey Ethell and Alfred Price, Sidgwick and Jackson Ltd.

Main Actions mentioned in text, during Falklands Conflict, May-June 1982

1. 1 May, Flt Lt Dave Morgan takes part in the attack on Port Stanley Airfield; claims an Islander destroyed, own Sea Harrier damaged.
2. 1 May, Lt Steve Thomas and Flt Lt Paul Barton shoot down two Mirages.
3. 9 May, Flt Lt Dave Morgan attacks the Argentine intelligence gathering trawler *Narwal.*
4. 21 May, Sqn Ldr Jerry Pook and Flt Lt Mark Hare destroy three Argentine helicopters on Mount Kent.
5. 21 May, Flt Lt Jeff Glover shot down near Port Howard, taken prisoner.
6. 21 May, Flt Lt Tony Harper takes part in armed reconnaissance of Dunnose Head airfield.
7. 21 May, Lt-Cdr 'Sharkey' Ward, accompanied by Lt Steve Thomas and Lt-Cdr Al Craig, shoots down a Pucara near Goose Green.
8. 21 May, Lt Steve Thomas and Lt-Cdr 'Sharkey' Ward shoot down three Daggers over West Falkland.
9. 23 May, Flt Lt Dave Morgan destroys two Argentine helicopters near Shag Cove, other pilots destroy one more.
10. 24 May, Flt Lt Tony Harper takes part in attack on Port Stanley Airfield.
11. 28 May, Flt Lt Tony Harper takes part in attack on Goose Green.
12. 1 June, Lt-Cdr 'Sharkey' Ward, accompanied by Lt Steve Thomas, shoots down a C-130 Hercules off Pebble Island.
13. 5 June, Flt Lt Tony Harper attacks Argentine troops near Sapper Hill.
14. 8 June, Flt Lt Dave Morgan and Lt Dave Smith destroy three Skyhawks over Choiseul Sound.
15. 13 June, Lt-Cdr Neil Thomas and Lt Simon Hargreaves make emergency landings on the decks of the assault ships *Fearless* and *Intrepid* in San Carlos Water.

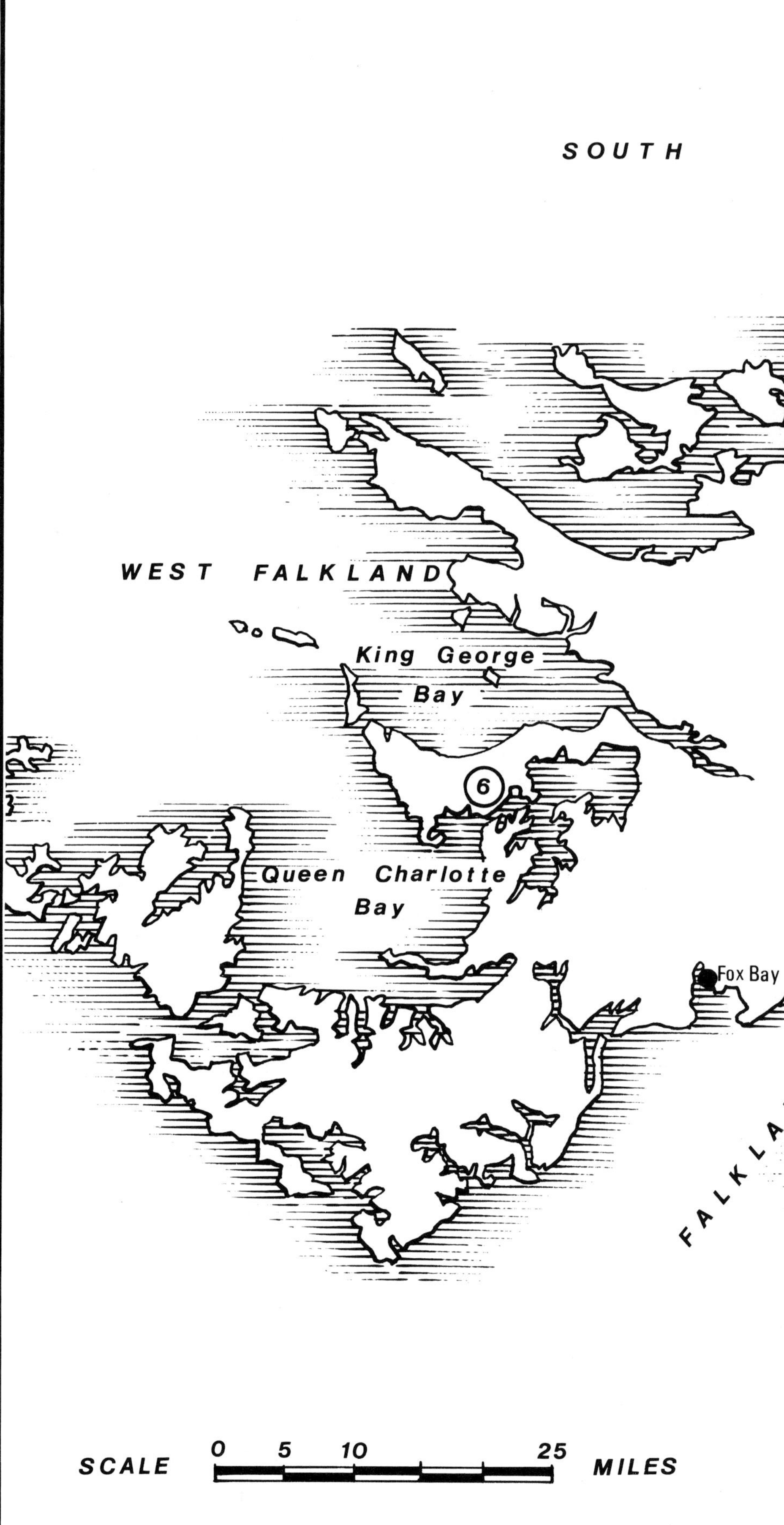

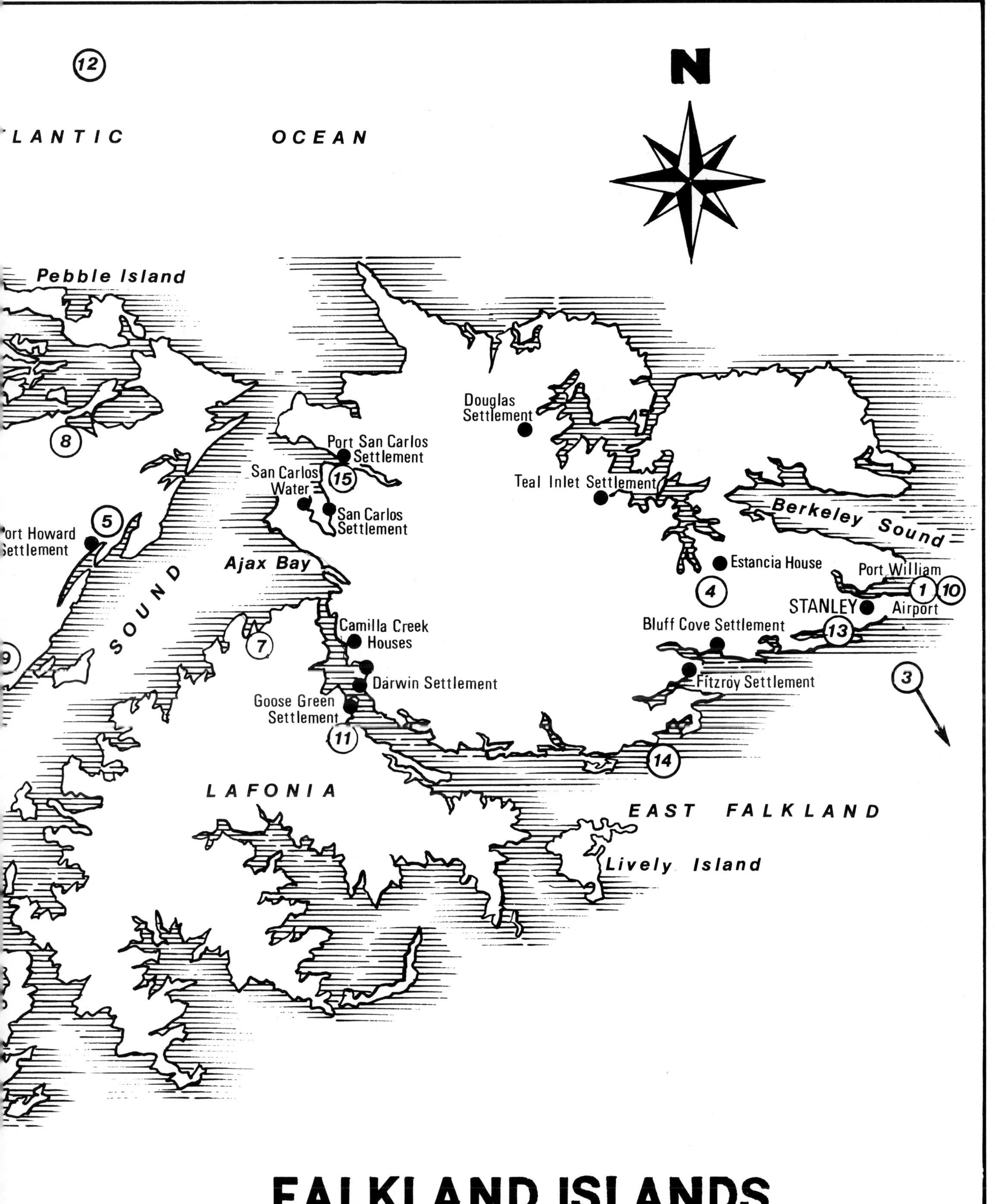

FALKLAND ISLANDS